HI-TECH
PLANES

HI-TECH PLANES

THE LATEST IN THE AIR WARFARE REVOLUTION

WAYNE F. GEER

Quantum
Books

A QUANTUM BOOK

This book is produced by
Quantum Publishing Ltd.
6 Blundell Street
London N7 9BH

Copyright ©MCMXCII
Quintet Publishing Limited.

This edition printed 2003

All rights reserved.
This book is protected by copyright. No part of it may be
reproduced, stored in a retrieval system, or transmitted in
any form or by any means, without the prior permission
in writing of the Publisher, nor be otherwise circulated in
any form of binding or cover other than that in which it
is published and without a similar condition including
this condition being imposed on the subsequent
publisher.

ISBN 1-86160-685-0

QUMHTP

Printed in Singapore by
Star Standard Industries Pte Ltd.

CONTENTS

GENERAL DYNAMICS F-111. 6
GRUMMAN F-14 TOMCAT 11
NORTHROP F/A-19 HORNET 18
McDONNELL DOUGLAS AV-8B HARRIER 22
McDONNELL DOUGLAS F-15 EAGLE 27
GENERAL DYNAMICS F-16 FIGHTING FALCON. 32
MIG-25 FOXBAT. 38
MIG-23 FLOGGER 41
MIG-29 FULCRUM 44
MIG-31 FOXHOUND 47
SU-27 FLANKER 50
B-1B BOMBER 53
B-2 STEALTH BOMBER 58
F-22 ADVANCED TACTICAL FIGHTER 62
YF-23 NORTHROP FIGHTER 68
F-117 STEALTH FIGHTER 72
V-22 OSPREY 76
SR-71 BLACKBIRD 80
AH-1 COBRA. 86
AH-64 APACHE 91
RAH-66 COMANCHE 96
PATRIOT AIR DEFENCE MISSILE 100
AGM-114 HELLFIRE MISSILE 103
AGM-65 MAVERICK MISSILE 106
AIM-120 AMRAAM 108
INDEX 110

GENERAL DYNAMICS F-111

The General Dynamics F-111 *Aardvark* was an aeroplane for all seasons, according to the men in the White House. It became 50 tonnes of controversy in the United States military establishment. It also became the first ground-attack aircraft capable of very low level penetration of hostile airspace able to plant a bomb within 50 metres (164 ft) of the target while flying blind. Even though it was designated as a fighter, it has never acted as a fighter, and in fact it never will do.

The F-111 grew out of the need to replace the Republic F-105 *Thunderchief* in the USAF and the F-4 *Phantom* in the US Navy. Both services were working out the design needs of their aircraft when Robert S. McNamara, Secretary of Defense, arrived in the seat of power to influence aircraft procurement. McNamara compelled the two services to accept an aircraft common to both with the minimum of changes for the Navy version. Production of the F-111B Navy model was eventually stopped in 1968, when the F-14 *Tomcat* programme began.

The role this new aeroplane was supposed to play was a controversial question during the development stage. The USAF wanted a ground-attack as well as a fighter plane, whereas the Navy needed a fleet-defence aircraft. A plane that could fill all roles was out of the question at the time, and the F-111 became an all-weather attack bomber with an internal bay for nuclear weapons. The ability to fly long-range missions at supersonic speed (Mach 1.2) using terrain-following radar became the primary role. The many thousands of planes some military leaders dreamed of being built stopped short of 562 examples, split among nine different models.

The VG (Variable Geometry) wing for the F-111 resulted from the work of the British Vickers research, data being supplied to the American John Stack. Mr Stack was chief of the supersonic wind tunnel at Langley Laboratory and became the leading authority on VG wings. When the advanced fighter design work was started, the VG wing was the only item in the Tactical Fighter Experimental request for bids. The variable-sweep wing was not a problem in the F-111's development, and indeed was a major reason for the plane's success.

▼ **An F-III waits for its pilot under a lowering sky. The F-III is an all-weather bomber.**

▲ **An F-111 flying over mountainous terrain, its variable geometry wings swept back.**

A variable geometry wing has certain advantages over a fixed wing. Among these is that while drag is greatly reduced as the wing is swept aft the wing area is only slightly reduced. This allows the F-111 to fly at Mach 1.2 at tree-top level. Also, the lift versus angle of attack of the wing is very flat with the wing sweep to 72.5 degrees. This allows the aircraft to have a much easier ride when flying in low-level turbulence than a long-winged plane would have, and this allows for very effective high-speed low-level attack missions to be undertaken.

One exceptional design item possessed by the F-111 is the crew ejection capsule in place of ejection seats. This gives much better protection for the crew on both land and water in case of loss of the plane. The capsule is severed from the plane by explosives, then driven clear by a 40,000-lb (18,000 kg) thrust rocket motor. Oxygen supply is maintained inside the capsule but pressure is lost. The ejection system works from maximum supersonic speed, zero altitude. The capsule has even kept a crew alive while rolling down a mountainside. The aircraft was also the first to be fitted with airbags, which are used to cushion touchdown of the capsule.

The F-111 is a long-range (without refuelling) aircraft. To achieve this, fuel is carried in every available space inside the plane. This massive fuel load and the heavy bomb load drove the weight to almost 54,500 kg (120,000 lb). The combination is also what gave the F-111 the greatest range/bomb load combination of any tactical strike aircraft in the West's inventory.

ENGINES

The F-111 required about 40,000 lb of thrust to maintain a cruising speed of Mach 1.2 at low altitude. The engines selected would have to operate from sea level up to 50,000 ft, (15,000 m) with long periods of supersonic speed at sea level. Two engines were required to meet the thrust requirement. The engine selected was the Pratt & Whitney TF-30. This may not have been the best choice, but it is the one the plane has had to live with.

The TF-30 is a afterburning turbofan engine of 20,000 lb thrust. Continued development until 1970 culminated in the development of the TF-30-P-100 engine of 30,000 lb thrust. Unfortunately, the USAF could not afford to purchase the newest engine, and the F-111 programme was cancelled. The remaining F-111s are still equipped with the older model engines.

TERRAIN-FOLLOWING RADAR

Blind, night, or bad-weather flying at low altitude demands the very best TF (Terrain-following) radar available. For the F-111, Texas Instruments supplies the APQ-110 system for the later model F-111F, and it is fitted retrospectively to older model planes.

The APQ-110 is a pair of TF radars, either one of which can be used as the primary system. The second can back-up the primary or sweep to the side to help the pilot in choosing a path to fly. In use, the TF mode keeps the aircraft on a level path until a calculated angle to clear an obstruction is reached, then sends a command to the autopilot to begin a pitch-up manoeuvre. The system makes the aircraft ride as if it is on a ski with an upturned tip, always pitching down as soon as it clears an obstruction and up again as soon as another obstruction comes within range of the forward tip.

The system also keeps track of side obstructions in case the pilot changes course, and when the aircraft banks the actual height above ground level is maintained. In event of malfunction a 2g pull-up is automatically executed. Flight at minimum AGL (height above ground level) and speed of Mach 1.2 has been demonstrated. It has been written that TF flight in the F-111 is terrifying until the pilot gets used to it.

AVIONICS

In addition to the TF radar equipment, the F-111 is equipped with a full range of communications, navigation, and ECM (Electronic Counter Measures) equipment. Litton AJQ-20A inertial bombing and navigation sub-system gives the plane a completely independent navigation system. One requirement is a precisely known starting point to set the inertial navigation system. The ballistics computer then guides the plane, with the aid of the main attack radar, to a precise drop point. For return to base the navigation system can guide the F-111 to touch down on an airport without external navigation radio aids – if the runway is exactly where someone said it was.

A variety of ECM and threat-detection devices are carried internally, and different pods are carried externally. Internally, there is a Sanders Associates ALQ-94, used for both noise and deception jamming. This device is effective against the Soviet SA-6 SAM. An up-dated version, the AJQ-134, is now being supplied to F-111 users. The F-111 carries an integrated warning system to detect all radar and IR (Infra Red) threats from all around the aircraft. The Dalmo-Victor APS-109A is the radar homing and warning system. To warn the F-111 of approaching missiles or aircraft, the Cincinnati Electronics AAR-34 and ALR-23 are carried.

▲ A flight of four EF and FB-111s.

◀ An FB-111 on takeoff with its wings forward and afterburner.

SPECIFICATION	
WINGSPAN:	
MAXIMUM:	1,005.84 cm (33 ft 0 in)
MINIMUM:	974.09 cm (31 ft 11½ in)
WINGSWEEP:	16° to 72½°
LENGTH:	2,302.51 cm (75 ft 6½ in)
HEIGHT:	519.43 cm (17 ft ½ in)
TAKEOFF WEIGHT: (A TO E)	41,413.68 kg (91,300 lb)
(FB-111A)	54,088.62 kg (119,243 lb)
ENGINES:	TP-30-P series
ENGINE THRUST:	18,500 lb up to 25,000 lb in P-100
MAXIMUM SPEED:	Mach 1.2 at sea level, Mach 2.2 above 35,000 ft
SERVICE CEILING:	Above 50,000 ft

HI-TECH PLANES

▲ F-111 dropping MK-82 practice bombs over the Nevada desert.

WEAPONS

The purpose of the F-111 is to deliver weapons, either nuclear or conventional. The aircraft has always had an internal weapons bay to carry two (or more) nuclear weapons a long distance and deliver them with precision. The supporting electronics are just to give the plane a better chance of success in the mission and returning to home base.

To deliver conventional weapons, the F-111 has internal bomb-bay space, external pylons on the fuselage and wings, and the M61A1 Vulcan cannon. The M61 is carried in the bomb bay along with 2,072 rounds of 20-mm ammunition and is not permanently mounted. Only the six inner wing pylons are used for bombs and, in operation, only the four inner pylons. The two outer pylons are used only for fuel tanks. This makes the maximum bomb load just under 9,100 kg (20,000 lb). The multiple ejection racks each carry stores in two groups of three bombs, giving a maximum of 24 bombs on the external racks. Total bomb loads up to 13,150 kg (29,000 lb) were carried aloft as early as the start of 1968. Bombing and navigation accuracy of the F-111 at that time was described as phenomenal, and eight times better than the next best fighter bomber in the USAF. Of course, each new aircraft has been able to make that claim as it is brought into service.

COMBAT

By March 1968 the US Air Force was anxious to put the new plane into combat in Vietnam. Six F-111s flew without drop tanks and without air refueling, using inertial navigation, to Thailand. On 28 March 1968, the first of three F-111s disappeared on combat flights. Fifty-five completely successful missions were flown with the loss of three aircraft. The crew of one of the lost aircraft had ejected and the wreckage of the plane was found. Inspection of the wreckage revealed that a weld had failed on the left tailplane and caused the crash. Another crash occurred in the USA the very next day due to the same tailplane failure.

Years later, F-111s flew all the way from England to Libya in an exercise aimed at deterring the use of terrorism by Col. Gadhafi.

The F-111 has suffered much abuse and criticism, and the plane has had many shortcomings. It is now a mature aeroplane – a strike, or attack, plane, not a fighter. For the role it plays as a long-range, night and bad-weather attack plane there is not another in the world that can match it.

GRUMMAN F-14 TOMCAT

The Grumman F-14 *Tomcat* is considered by many people in the aviation community to be the best all-around fighter interceptor in the world. When it was first introduced, it certainly was the best, and it is still among the very top interceptors in use today.

In February 1961 Secretary of Defense Robert McNamara recommended that the US Air Force and the US Navy develop a single aeroplane into two models, one for each service. The common design concept was supposed to be a major cost-saving operation. Instead, in 1968 the US Navy cancelled the programme and was no closer to developing the much needed replacement aircraft for the ageing F-4 *Phantom* II.

In 1965 the Navy had provided funding to the Grumman Company for advanced fighter studies. With the pending demise of the Navy F-111B, Grumman proposed a different plane based on the F-111 weapons control system and engines. This design went through several evolutionary stages, the VFX (Experimental Fighter) competition with the other US aircraft manufacturers, and became the Navy's F-14A *Tomcat*.

Lamentably, on its very first flight, the first prototype F-14A suffered complete hydraulic systems failure and crashed one mile short of the runway. Both pilots ejected seconds before the impact. The crash was shown on national television news that same evening. The cause of the crash was failure of two titanium hydraulic oil lines, and the remedy was to replace both lines with stainless steel. A second aircraft went through extensive testing of the hydraulic systems and began flight operations in May 1971.

STRUCTURE

The F-14 variable-sweep wing was a carry-over from the F-111 programme and gives the *Tomcat* much of its flight capability. Usually the sweep is computer-controlled and depends on the airspeed.

▼ **An F-14 *Tomcat* leaves the carrier.**

▲ **An F-14 about to land aboard a carrier. The 20 mm cannon has been in recent use.**

Other modes of sweep control secure the wing at 55 degrees for surface attack combat, or the pilot can manually sweep the wing for maximum acceleration. There is also an emergency system to bring the wings forward for landing. With the wing fully extended, the pilot has good visibility over the nose for carrier landing. Small glove vanes set in the leading area of the wing glove are automatically extended at supersonic speed to reduce the aerodynamic stability of the plane. These small vanes allow the F-14 to hold a 7.7g turn at speeds from Mach 2.0 down to Mach 1.0.

The F-14 does not use conventional ailerons for roll control. Instead, the all-moving "tailerons" provide both pitch and roll control. Below Mach 1, spoilers on the wings provide additional roll control. Pilot control is through the tried and proven spring-and-bobweight system, not fly-by-wire. Control augmentation and stability systems, as well as automatic control, are installed and are normally in use. But the pilot can still fly the plane without the electronic control systems.

The fuselage of the F-14 has the two engines set as far apart as possible. The area between the long, straight engine pods acts as a low-aspect wing and provides much of the lift needed by the plane. The fighter has been flown at very high angles of attack with the wing stalled and only the body lift holding it in the air. The control surfaces and the variable-sweep wing combine to give the F-14 *Tomcat* excellent flight agility – enough agility to allow it to remain one of the very best fighter interceptors in the world.

POWER PLANT

Power for the *Tomcat* comes from two General Electric TP-30-P-12 engines, originally developed for the F-111B project. It was known at the time that this engine was not fully suitable for the F-14 and new engines were under development. The Advanced Technology Engines (ATE) never arrived, and the F-14 has had to use two derivatives, the P-414 and the P-414A, until some time into the 1990s when the F110-GE-400 will come into fleet service.

The TP-30 is an afterburning turbofan engine which develops just under 21,000 lb thrust. This amount of thrust gives the *Tomcat* only about 0.78 per cent of aircraft thrust/weight unity, but still allows it to outperform the F-4 *Phantom* in all respects. All parties concede that the engines are not as good as desired, and that there has been trouble with them. The new engines are expected to remove all of the problems and performance deficiencies.

The Navy had been testing the ATE engine in the form of the Pratt & Whitney F-401 as early as 1970. The F-401 was rated at 28,000 lb thrust, almost a one-third increase in power. This engine development was suspended in 1974 due to the escalating cost of the F-14 programme, and because the F-14 seemed to be doing so well with the lower-cost engine. By 1976, study for a replacement engine focused on three models: the Pratt & Whitney F-401, the General Electric F-101-X and the Allison TF-41. The General Electric engine of about 28,000 lb thrust was eventually selected and will power most F-14s for some time into the 1990s.

▼ **A bottom view of the F-14 *Tomcat*, displaying an array of six AIM-54 *Phoenix* missiles – four underneath the body and two on wing pylons – capable of attacking six target simultaneously.**

AVIONICS AND ELECTRONICS

When the F-14 was designed it had to contend with Soviet aircraft such as the MIG-25, a 3,220 km/h (2,000 mph) interceptor with unknown capabilities, and with low-flying cruise or air-launched anti-shipping missiles. To achieve the desired interception abilities, the Airborne Weapons Group Nine (AWG-9) attack and detection system was selected. The AWG-9 system and the *Phoenix* AIM-54 missile are both built by Hughes Aircraft Company. What sets this system apart is its ability to track 24 separate targets simultaneously.

The AWG-9 system had *Sidewinder*, *Sparrow* and Vulcan cannon control ability added to it for the F-14. The AWG-9 system had been originally developed for the F-108, then continued for the F-111B. It reached full development in the F-14 *Tomcat* as an integrated system whose primary function is long-range detection of enemy targets and guidance of the *Phoenix* missile.

The system also uses coherent-pulse Doppler radar, which allows the computer to ignore clutter and project only moving objects onto the screen. This gives the F-14 a look-down, shoot-down capa-

bility to intercept low-flying aircraft or missiles. The system also has multi-mode operation in order to detect and track targets anywhere within the search area, such as high closure rate and low closure rate, or right-angle track to the plane.

All of this information is fed to the crew through computers which display on a group of VDT screens in both the front and back seat. A Tactical Information Display is the primary screen for situation display. The crew member in the back seat has a vital role in the defence of the plane and in attacking targets. He can launch *Phoenix* and *Sparrow* missiles, but only the pilot can launch the *Sidewinders*.

Another valuable system is the infra-red sensor mounted forward on the underside of the fuselage. This passive sensor can be used in conjunction with the radar or by itself. It can be used to feed information to *Sparrow* or *Sidewinder* missiles to aid in firing solutions as well as to search for IR sources at long range. With the new developments in IR technology, this equipment will continue to improve and become more important in detecting hostile weapons.

WEAPONS

The F-14 is a weapons system, and the real reason for the *Tomcat* was the AWG-9/AIM-54 *Phoenix* missile system and the built-in M61A1 20-mm cannon system. The *Phoenix* missile system was designed to control up to six missiles attacking six separate targets at the same time. The system will also track 24 separate targets. This capability was demonstrated and the F-14 has been accepted as a superb weapons system for the fleet-defence role.

The F-14 can carry up to 6,577 kg (14,500 lb) of

▲ An F-14 *Tomcat* climbing away from the carrier.

external weapons load, but only the common iron bomb is certified for air-to-ground use. The *Phoenix* AIM-54 is unique to the F-14 and is the primary weapon for air-to-air fleet-defence use. The AIM-54 was designed to arm the Navy F-111B and was developed from the earlier AIM-47 missile that was to arm the Mach 3.2 F-108 *Rapier* interceptor.

The AIM-54 is a large missile at 396.24 cm (13 ft) long, 38.1 cm (15 in) in diameter, weighing 442.26 kg (975 lb) with a 59.87-kg (132-lb) fragmentation warhead. The warhead is detonated by any one of three means: a direct hit fuse, a proximity fuse or an IR fuse. The maximum speed of the missile may be up to Mach 5 at high altitude or Mach 3.8 at lower altitude. The *Phoenix* is a climb-and-dive missile. That is, it climbs during the first part of its travel, then dives towards the target. This maintains flight energy during the terminal part of its travel. The missile will climb above 100,000 ft on a long-range intercept.

Two prime targets for the F-14 *Tomcats* are the MiG-25 and the new Soviet *Backfire* bomber. Test launches of the *Phoenix* were carried out with target aircraft simulating the Soviet aircraft. The tests were completely successful and multiple intercepts were subsequently attempted. Target aircraft doing 6g pullout from a dive were successfully intercepted. A target flying at Mach 1.5 at 50,000 ft was intercepted at 116 km (72 miles) by the *Phoenix* at a launch range of 188 km (110 miles). Violently manoeuvring targets were also intercepted by the *Phoenix*. The *Phoenix* AIM-54 is now being upgraded to the AIM-54C version, which is an improved missile, not a new design.

◄ A US Navy F-14 *Tomcat* flies over the desert having launched from a carrier on a combat mission during Operation Desert Shield – the main operation of the 1991 Gulf War.

Although the *Phoenix* is the primary weapon for the F-14, others are carried to supplement the weapons load. The AIM-9 *Sidewinder* and the AIM-7 *Sparrow* are shorter-range weapons, and are usually mixed in with the *Phoenix* load. Also, their cost is much less than the *Phoenix* and there are larger stocks. The Hughes AMRAAM AIM-120 will be a future stock missile to arm the F-14 *Tomcat*. The M61 Vulcan cannon with 675 rounds of ammunition gives the *Tomcat* lethal short-range claws. As with most M61 Vulcan cannons, the maximum rate of fire is 6,000 rounds per minute.

PERFORMANCE AND HANDLING

The F-14 was the first in a line of modern US air superiority fighter planes. It was designed for the US Navy, and the Navy required two crew members. The variable geometry (VG) wing was selected to give the fighter the manoeuvrability it required at all flight speeds. The F-14 had been designed by Grumman to be a nearly spin-proof fighter, but this condition was not achieved for years. The plane would enter a fast, flat spin from which recovery was not possible. A programme to correct this flight problem was initiated in 1980, and only a gradual series of solutions was found. Today, the F-14 is nearly spin-proof.

Overspending and funding problems hampered the F-14 programme from the start and prevented the proper engines from being selected for years. That short-sightedness has now been corrected. The top speed, ceiling, and rate of climb are similar to that of the older F-4 *Phantom II* but the F-14 is a much superior plane. When air-to-air combat between these two airplanes begins, the F-14 outperforms the F-4 by a wide margin. The *Phantom* simply cannot stay with the F-14 and ends up as a target. The two crew members and the VG wings make up for any other shortcomings, and the US Navy has an essential fleet-defence weapon in the F-14 *Tomcat*.

▼ **An F-14 *Tomcat* prepares to launch from the carrier.**

▶ **A flight of five Tomcats.**

SPECIFICATION	
WINGSPAN:	
MAXIMUM:	1,954.53 cm (64 ft 1½ in)
MINIMUM:	1,164.59 cm (38 ft 2½ in)
LENGTH:	1,910.06 cm (62 ft 8 in)
HEIGHT:	487.68 cm (16 ft)
ENGINES:	Two General Electric F-110-GE-400
ENGINE THRUST:	28,000 lb
MAXIMUM SPEED:	Mach 2.5 above 35,000 ft
SERVICE CEILING:	Above 50,000 ft

NORTHROP F/A-18 HORNET

The F/A-18 *Hornet* was seven years in the design and testing. Although criticized for not being big enough, expensive enough, or able to do everything the F-14 *Tomcat* is capable of, the F/A-18 is an ideal aeroplane for the time and mission for which it is being procured.

The F/A-18 is an outgrowth of the Light Weight Fighter (LWF) competition between the YF-16 and the YF-17, which was awarded to the General Dynamics F-16 aircraft. The Northrop YF-17 was not selected because of only minor deficiencies and was actually superior to the YF-16 in some respects. For example, the YF-17 had a better turn rate at a speed of Mach 0.9. The YF-16 was superior at other airspeeds. This left the Northrop Company with an excellent fighter design, and nowhere to go with it.

In 1974 the US Navy (which had dropped out of the LWF programme) sent out a Request for Proposal for a lightweight multi-role fighter to be based on aircraft carriers. The proposed fighter would replace the F-4 *Phantom*, the A-4 *Skyhawk* and the A-7 *Corsair* as a fleet-defence and surface-attack airplane. Northrop teamed with McDonnell Douglas for their carrier plane expertise to redesign the YF-17 to meet the Navy's carrier requirement. The resulting F/A-18A was a new design, and not a loser from some other competition. In May 1975 the F/A-18 was selected by the Navy for its new fighter/attack airplane.

The redesign work to make the plane suit carriers and multi-role applications caused the weight to increase. This led to 4.65 sq m (50 sq ft) of surface area being added to the wing. Increased weight demanded more power, and the improved General Electric F-404 engines were installed. This engine had been under development for the YF-17 but had not been available at that time. With the redesign and higher cost came a longer service life of 6,000 hours and 2,000 carrier launches and recoveries. Also, ease of maintenance was of prime consideration in the design.

During the flight test and evaluation, a number of shortcomings were found in the fighter. These involved range, acceleration, and rate of

▼ The F/A-18 Hornet night attack prototype makes a test flight above Missouri farms outisde of St. Louis. Night attack F/A-18s are equipped with an infra-red navigation system, called a Thermal Imaging Navigation Set (TINS).

roll. One by one each problem was identified and solved. Sometimes more than one problem was overcome with one solution. For example, the rate of roll was improved by resizing the ailerons, and this also reduced the approach (to the carrier) landing speed. During carrier qualification a landing gear failed, resulting in damage to the plane and a minor redesign to cure the problem.

During flight testing it was found that the F/A-18 is almost immune to spinning. However, one aircraft was lost due to entering a spin from which it could not recover. At least 110 test flights were flown to duplicate the conditions that led to the spin and in short order the problem was solved. A "spin button" was added to the flight computer which gave the pilot full authority over control-surface movement. A cockpit display of the required control-stick position for recovery was added to an existing CRT in the cockpit. The computer was later reprogrammed and the need for a switch on the stick was eliminated.

▶ Designed for one-man operation, the F/A-18's cockpit makes use of the latest computer technology to keep pilot aware of the situation at all times. Information is shown to pilots on three multipurpose colour displays and a heads-up display.

◀ A Canadian CF-18 Hornet races skyward above a frosty landscape. Canada became the first international F/A-18 customer when it purchased 138 strike fighters in 1980.

CONTROLS

The control surfaces on the *Hornet* are a combination of quadruple fly-by-wire (FBW) with electrical back-up to all controls, and a final direct mechanical back-up to the all-flying stabilators. The wing flaps, leading-edge slats and ailerons work together through the flight computer to give the wing a continuously variable camber. This provides the aerofoil shape needed throughout the flight envelope, and provides optimum performance. The FBW system allows the pilot freedom to fly as he wishes and not to have to guard against exceeding aircraft flight limits, although the computer can be overridden by the pilot in combat.

COCKPIT

McDonnell Douglas started from scratch when they began the F/A-18 cockpit design. The end result is a very clean and uncluttered pilot station. A variety of computer controls and displays help to handle the work load, and the pilot keeps his hands on the throttle and stick. The Heads Up Display shows most of the information needed by the pilot, calling for only a quick glance at one of the three CRT displays to get additional information.

RADAR AND SENSORS

The radar carried by the F/A-18 is the APG-65, a coherent-pulse Doppler type. It operates in the 8 to 12.6 GHz range and is standard for fighter aircraft. The Doppler effect allows the radar to pick out a moving target against the ground clutter. This radar has various modes of operation, and is tied in with the computers to display threat aircraft and give the pilot firing solutions based on the weapon of choice. Built-in test equipment also tests the radar and all of the avionics.

For attack at night and during bad weather, the F/A-18 can be equipped with Forward Looking Infra-Red and Laser Spot Tracking pods in place of the two inboard *Sparrow* missiles. The FLIR pod provides a TV picture to the pilot, and to the computers. The computer then gives a weapon-firing solution to the pilot depending on the weapon of choice. The laser can be used to mark a target for another aircraft, or lock on and track a target for the carrying aircraft. This method of designating a target for a second aircraft is used by several different fighters as well as attack helicopters.

POWER PLANTS

The original YF-17A was powered by two of the General Electric JY-101 low-bypass turbojet engines. This engine developed 15,000 lb of static thrust. General Electric was also developing the F-404 engine, and it became available to handle the increased demands of the F/A-18. The F-404 engine is a turbofan with a bypass ratio of 0.34. The bypass air is used to cool the engine and reduces the need for outside cooling air. This engine develops 16,000 lb of thrust, the same power as the J-79 engine that drives the F-104 *Starfighter*. The F/A-18 *Hornet* carries two of these highly reliable engines.

WEAPONS

In the fighter role, the F/A-18 comes equipped with the standard M61A1 Vulcan 20 mm six-barrel cannon with 570 rounds of ammunition in a rotary drum. Unlike most other aircraft, the F/A-18 has the cannon mounted in the nose on the centre-line. The fire and smoke debris from firing the cannon do not bother the pilot or reduce visibility through the windscreen. The nose-mounted radar unit is shock mounted in order to prevent the shock of firing the cannon from damaging it. No problem has been reported with the radar as a result of this installation.

For missiles the F/A-18 carries an AIM-9 *Sidewinder* on each wing tip, and the AIM-7F *Sparrow*. The AIM-120 advanced short-range missile has been test fired from the F/A-18, and is expected to arm the fighter in the future.

For surface attack (ground and water), a wide choice of arms is available. For precision attack of any hard target, the MK82 970-kg (2,000-lb) laser-guided bomb can be used, or the *Maverick* missile in ground and anti-ship versions. To attack hostile radar units, the HARM (High Speed Anti Radiation) missile is carried. The *Harpoon*, a long-range (109 km or 68 mile) anti-shipping weapon may be selected for a stand-off attack against a hostile fleet.

▼ **A US Navy Hornet prepares for a catapult launch from the deck of its carrier. The first aircraft carrier deployment for the F/A-18 took place on board the Constellation in 1985. Hornets flew about one third of US Navy sorties during the course of the Gulf War.**

▲ An F/A-18 loaded for the ground attack role. Sidewinder air-to-air missiles, along with the internal 20mm cannon, provide air-to-air capability and the large fuel tank will give a longer loiter time.

SPECIFICATION	
Wingspan:	1,143 cm (37 ft 6 in)
Length:	1,706.88 cm (56 ft)
Height:	466.09 cm (15 ft 3½ in)
Engines:	Two General Electric F-404 Turbofans
Engine Thrust:	16,000 lb
Maximum Speed:	Above 36,000 ft, Mach 1.8+
Service Ceiling:	Above 50,000 ft

The maximum weight of this external weapons load is reported to be 7,711 kg (17,000 lb). With air refuelling, this maximum amount of ordnance can be loaded on the fighter and can be carried into battle.

PERFORMANCE

The F/A-18 *Hornet* is credited with an airspeed of Mach 1.8+ above 36,000 ft, and an initial climb rate of 50,000 ft per minute. This is just about equal to the capability of the F-16 *Fighting Falcon*. The only real superiority of the F-16 is in sustained turns. A combat between these two fighters will most likely be won by the fighter that detects the other one first. This has become the guiding light of all fighter engagements today, and has led to the combat control and communications special aeroplanes development such as the *Hawkeye* and Boeing 707 Command and Control plane.

The F/A-18 *Hornet* has evolved into a superior multi-role aircraft able to excel at any mission. With excellent maintainability, flexible weapon load ability, and superior air-to-air fighter ability the F/A-18 *Hornet* will be with us well into 21st century.

▼ An F/A-18 strike fighter pilot breaks away from his wingman. Both planes are carrying two heat-seeking Sidewinder missiles and a 330 gallon external fuel tank.

McDONNELL DOUGLAS AV-8B HARRIER

The AV-8B *Harrier:* invented by the French, developed by the British, given to the Americans. It is the only successful VTOL (Vertical Take Off Landing) fixed-wing aircraft in the British and American inventory, and is a very fine plane for the role it operates in.

The concept of vertical lift was proposed by the French designer Michel Wibault in 1956. When neither the French nor US Air Forces were interested, he took the concept to the Mutual Weapons Development Program (MWDP), a USA-funded programme to help develop promising European weapons. Wibault and Gordon Lewis filed the first patent on a *Harrier*-like aeroplane in that same year. The beauty of the Wibault design was the simplicity of a single engine with four nozzles that rotate through 90° for both lift and thrust, at a time when other designs were using up to nine engines in one aircraft. The first aircraft designation for the Wibault design was P1127.

This engine also had counter-rotating high- and low-pressure compressors to eliminate torque, and plenum-chamber-burning (PCB). PCB augments thrust in the same way that afterburning does in a non-vectored thrust engine. The Bristol Company carried the development into the first *Pegasus* engine, which first ran in September 1959. The *Pegasus 2* engine became a real turbofan, and was first run in 1960.

During the 1960s, British and French politics vascillated with the result that military systems suffered at every turn. The P1127 survived by being mostly company funded and was first flown in vertical takeoff on 21 October, 1960. On 2 July, 1961 the second aircraft was flown in conventual mode. Low-level speed of over 500 knots, 6g turns, altitude of over 40,000 ft and supersonic flight of Mach 1.2 in a shallow dive were quickly attained. An improved version the *Kestrel*, was developed and the test/development programme continued with the British Air Staff writing a requirement for a simple attack and reconnaissance plane to replace an early *Hunter* aircraft. This requirement led to the development of the *Harrier* as a combat aircraft.

Six developmental aircraft were built as combat planes with the structure designed and built to handle the stress of 3,000 hours of low-level, high-speed flying. Engine power increased to keep up with weight, and eventually allowed up to 3,628 kg (8,000 lb) of bomb load to be carried on the AV-8A model.

▼ **Three AV-8Bs from the Marine Corps Air Station at Cherry Point, North Carolina, fly in formation above the western US Sierra Nevada mountains.**

▲ **A Marine Corps AV-8B practises a short takeoff during forward site operations.**

ENGINE

The *Pegasus* engine is unique in aviation. It is a turbofan with the forward fans mounted in front of the front engine bearing. All of the fan blades touch each other by snubbers mounted on the blades. This arrangement, along with vibration tuning, keeps the natural resonant frequency outside of the RPM range of the engine. There are three stages of low-pressure fan compression, and the compressed air is ducted through the forward nozzles as cold air and used for lift and thrust. The high-pressure hot gasses are ducted through the rear nozzles.

Control of the four nozzles is critical for vectored thrust through 90.5° of rotation. To achieve absolute control of all four nozzles, high-pressure air at 400°C is bled from the HP compressor to two air motors driving a differential gearbox. A shaft goes to each end of the engine to a cross-shaft. On each end of the cross-shaft is a chain to drive the angle of the nozzle. If either air motor fails, the second drives the unit at half speed. The nozzles can be driven at up to 100° per second, and the system has proven to be reliable and accurate.

While the British were improving the aircraft the US Marine Corps was watching developments. The Marines had been looking for new, good tactical fighters for years, and at the 1968 Farnborough Air Show they decided on the *Harrier*. General Leonard C. Chapman, Commandant of the Corps, ordered that this aircraft be evaluated for USMC service. As a result, 114 of the new aircraft were purchased. Shortly afterwards the AV-8A was licensed to be built in the USA by the McDonnell Douglas Company while it was also being produced in Britain.

Operational flying was begun in Europe in 1970 with a series of exercises designed to test dispersed-site operations. Four to twelve simulated combat missions were flown each day by each aircraft without benefit of an airfield. It was soon realized that a short take off (STO) was a much better way to operate than the vertical take off. Much greater loads of fuel and weapons could be carried in this way.

The technique for a STO is very simple. A "bug" on the airspeed indicator is set to a preselected airspeed and a nozzle angle stop is set to 50%. When the aircraft is lined up for takeoff the engine is run up to about 50% with the brakes locked. The throttle is advanced to 100% and the brakes released at the same time. As the airspeed indicator moves past the bug, the nozzle control is jerked back to the angle stop. Nozzle rotation is completed in less than half a second and the plane climbs out on the combination of vectored thrust and wing-generated lift. As the airspeed increases, the nozzles are slowly rotated to the full aft position. The *Harrier* has more thrust than weight and very great acceleration. It is reported that it is actually simpler to fly than most other attack aircraft.

The *Harrier* can be operated from small pads, ships or other unprepared sites. For landing on any surface other than a clean and dry one it is best to make a rolling landing at about 40 knots. This is to minimize the chance of foreign object damage (FOD) and to prevent hot gasses from being sucked into the engine.

▼ **A TAV-8B two-seat trainer climbs through the skies over St. Louis. The front cockpit, where the student sits, is identical to that of an AV-8B.**

WEAPONS

As an attack aircraft the AV-8A *Harrier* is certified to carry almost all external weapons in the inventory. It is armed with two 30 mm gun pods with 150 rounds per gun in two fuselage pods. There are four wing pylons that can carry almost anything up to 900-kg (2,000-lb) bombs. An additional centreline point can also carry everything except the multiple-ejection rack stores. Anti-ship missiles are also carried.

AIR COMBAT

Contrary to popular belief, the practice of VIFFing (Vector In Forward Flight) was not used by the British Pilots. It is reported to have been tried only slightly by a few daring pilots. This changed in 1970 when USMC Captain Harry Blot began testing the *Harrier* in air-combat manoeuvres. Captain Blot pushed the aircraft up to 500 knots and slammed the nozzle control to the 98-degree limit. As a result, Blot was slammed up against the stick as the plane violently decelerated – seat belts would be tight the next time.

During testing both in the aircraft and in computer simulators it was proved that this small, odd-shaped aircraft is hard to see, and can manoeuvre as no other aircraft can. It can suddenly slow down, and with the low-speed control jets can turn faster than anything. The USMC had British Aerospace (formally Hawker Siddeley) modify the power drive, strengthen the nozzles and install a screw-in temperature control fuse to allow 2½ minutes of full power instead of 75% in flight. This allowed the pilot to vector the thrust to any degree, at any speed, altitude or attitude. The results are described by the pilots as WILD.

Lt. Cdr. Doug Taylor, Royal Navy, wrote his thesis on the subject on an upward slope at the end of a short takeoff surface. The vertical component would give the STO aircraft the ability to carry a heavier load and allow greater time to react in the event of an emergency. There was little support in the British military for the so-called ski-jump. In 1976 the first government funded ski-jumps were constructed to study the idea.

With no modifications to the aeroplane a jump angle of 20° was achieved. This gave a 4g vertical acceleration, enough to carry 5,896.8 kg (13,000 lb) of fuel and weapons from only 182.88 m (600 ft) of rolling distance. Along with this development was the addition of the *Sea Harrier* model to the RN, just in time for the Falkland Islands operation.

In 1982 it became apparent that an armed conflict between the British forces and Argentina was imminent. The only sea aviation power possessed by the British Government was a handful of the *Harrier*

▼ **A Marine Corps AV-8B releases two high-drag Mk.82 Snakeye bombs above the Nevada desert during an exercise at the Naval Air Station at Fallon. The AV-8B is equipped with an angle rate bombing system that is one of the most accurate in the world.**

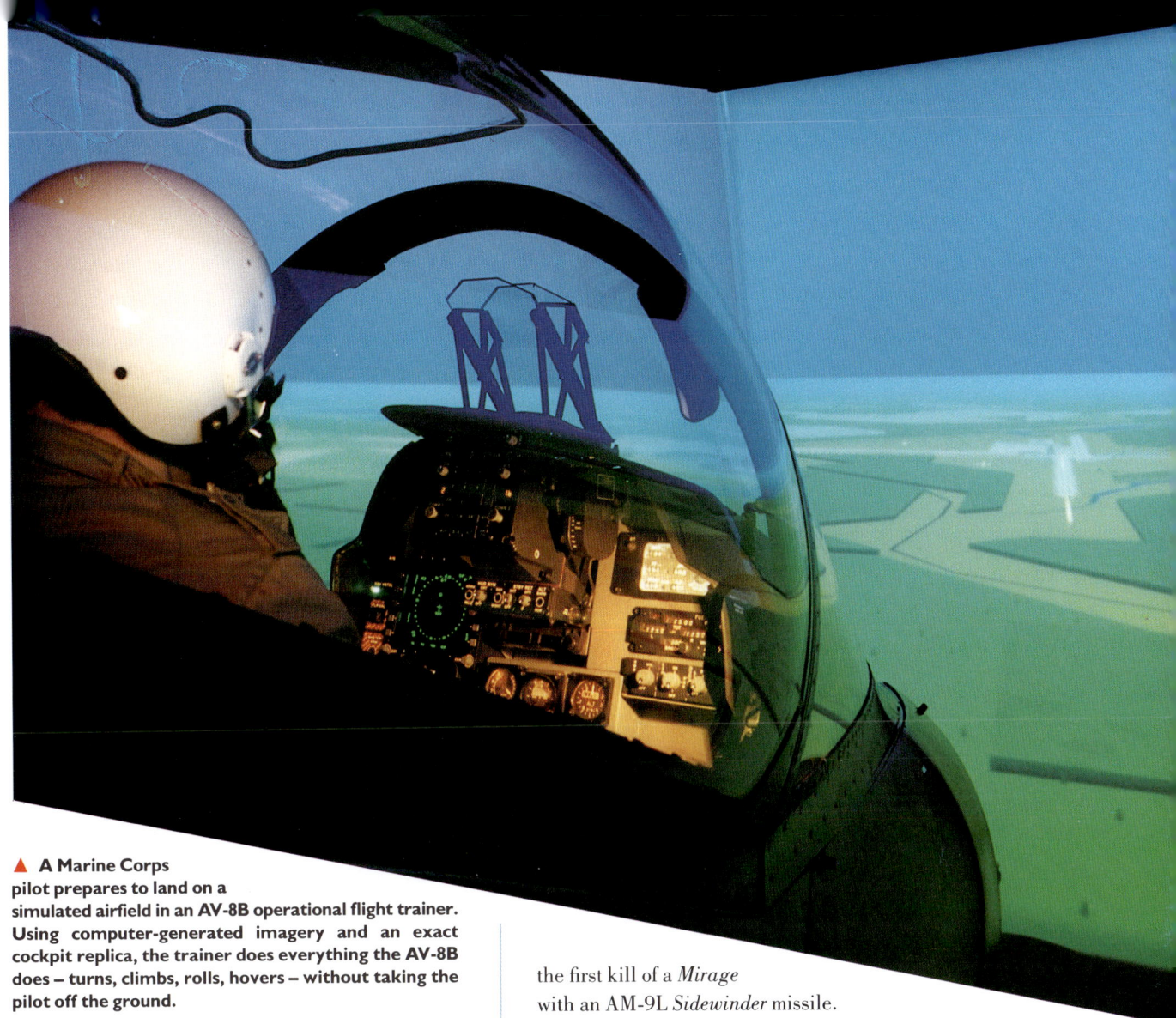

▲ **A Marine Corps pilot prepares to land on a simulated airfield in an AV-8B operational flight trainer. Using computer-generated imagery and an exact cockpit replica, the trainer does everything the AV-8B does – turns, climbs, rolls, hovers – without taking the pilot off the ground.**

and *Sea Harrier* aircraft. A total of 28 *Harriers* was all that could be rounded up to support the operation. Pilots were just as short, and at least two Royal Air Force pilots were drafted into the naval operation to man the aircraft. Some *Harriers* were flown all the way to Ascension Island with air-to-air refuelling (14 refuellings) by pilots who had never before done it. It is a great tribute to the Royal Navy and the pilots that the aircraft were modified, flown and transported in such a short time over such a great distance to carry out the task of air defence and ground attack in such a new aircraft. Air defence had not been foreseen, or planned for, in the development of the *Harrier*.

The first contact occurred on 25 April when a *Sea Harrier* intercepted an Argentine Boeing 707 on a long-range reconnaissance mission. The rules of combat did not allow the *Harrier* to fire on the 707. The first combat flights took place on 1 May with 12 *Harriers* attacking ground targets, and top air cover provided by other *Harriers*. At least four air interceptions were made that day, with *Harriers* evading long-range enemy air-to-air missiles. The *Harriers* scored at least three confirmed kills and three probable kills. F/Lt. Paul Barton, RAF, scored the first kill of a *Mirage* with an AM-9L *Sidewinder* missile.

The first *Harrier* was lost in action on 4 May when Lt. Nick Taylor was killed by AAA at Goose Green. On 20 May the RAF units began heavy ground-attack missions. Three more aircraft were lost to ground fire that month without pilot loss. One pilot, F/Lt. Jeffrey Glover, became the only British POW during the campaign. Ground fire and damage was so intense that the availability of the *Harrier* force was reduced to below "99.9%" of that of the *Sea Harrier* force. Only the finest aircraft could fight this hard and still have such a high availability rate of 95%!

Sea Harriers were assigned the Combat Air Patrol role, while RAF units handled the ground-attack duties. During the operation Corporate the *Sea Harriers* alone flew 2,376 missions, logging 2,675 hours of flying time. The start of the heaviest air war was on 21 May, Argentine Navy Day. Five Argentine A-4s were shot down, four with *Sidewinders* and one with guns. On 24 May three *Mirages* were shot down, and one crashed during evasive manoeuvres. Twenty-three aircraft kills, and three probables, were attributed to *Sea Harriers* during the operation. The *Harrier* was confirmed in hard combat as a first-class attack and air defence airplane.

▲ **An AV-8B
from Marine Attack Squadron 331
practices low-level flying over the Nevada desert during
training exercises.**

THE HARRIER II

McDonnell Aircraft joined Hawker in 1976 in a joint programme to produce the AV-8A *Harrier*. In 1975 the British government declined to continue the programme, leaving the US to develop the next version of the *Harrier*. This has led to two planes joining the line, the *Harrier II* and the *Harrier II Plus*. The new models are significantly improved planes with 15% larger supercritical wings, greater fuel capacity and the improved Rolls-Royce *Pegasus* 11-61 engine. The use of composite material reduced the weight of the wing alone by 136 kg (300 lb). Lift improvement devices have substantially improved vertical takeoff and landing performance.

The new engine provides 23,500 lb of thrust for better takeoff and a rated speed of Mach 0.92. Up to 6,003.4 kg (13,235 lb) of external ordnance can now be carried. The two cannons have been replaced by a single nose-mounted 25 mm cannon. The cockpit is now as modern as any fighter with Heads Up Display, Hands On Throttle and Stick, and new combat radar and fire control equipment.

SPECIFICATION

WINGSPAN:	923.54 cm (30 ft 4 in)
LENGTH:	1,411.22 cm (46 ft 4 in)
HEIGHT:	353.57 cm (11 ft 7 in)
MAXIMUM WEIGHT:	14,061.6 kg (31,000 lb)
ENGINE:	Rolls-Royce *Pegasus II*
ENGINE THRUST:	21.450 lb
MAXIMUM SPEED:	570 knots at sea level
	Mach 0.91 at altitude
SERVICE CEILING:	50,000 ft

There are eight wing store stations and one fuselage station that can carry a wide variety of weapons. The *Harrier* now has capability to carry laser-guided weapons such as the *Maverick* and guided smart bombs. Fifteen Mk-82 bombs can be carried, or a combination up to the maximum weight limit. Inside, 3,519.5 kg (7,759 lb) of fuel can be carried, with external tanks available. With air-to-air refuelling, the range is limited only by the pilot's physical ability.

The *Harrier* has proven itself to be one of the best single-seat, single-engine tactical attack aircraft in the world today. The dreams of the French designer Michel Wibault and all of the other early proponents have been well fulfilled by its success.

McDONNELL DOUGLAS F-15 EAGLE

The design for America's premier fighter, the F-15 *Eagle*, was started during the Vietnam War when a replacement for the F-4 *Phantom II* became necessary. The requirements were for a cannon- and missile-armed fighter to achieve air superiority over the Soviet MiGs in the sky above North Vietnam. The F-4 had been hard pressed to adequately defend itself and the other bombers flying combat missions at the time. The F-15 achieved air superiority, not over Vietnam, but over the skies of the Middle East in the 1980s and retained it during the Iraq/Kuwait Gulf conflict in 1990–91.

In 1965 the US Air Force began serious design and mission-statement work on a new fighter aircraft. This was the FX (Fighter-Experimental) designed as a single-service air superiority fighter, with engine power and flight agility to overcome any known or projected Soviet fighter. A Concept Formulation Study (CFS) was not awarded to McDonnell Douglas (the eventual F-15 contractor) at that time, and none of the proposed designs by the other manufacturers was given much further consideration. In 1967 a second Request For Proposal (RFP) was made and McDonnell Douglas, along with General Dynamics, was awarded the six-month study.

A Development Concept Paper (DCP) issued by the USAF included a speed range of Mach 1.5 to Mach 3.0 for a single-seat, twin-engine design weighing approximately 18,000 kg (40,000 lb). The FX designation was also changed to F-15, and the USAF began to defend the design against the US Navy. The Navy wanted the USAF to accept a modified version of the VFAX/F-14 *Tomcat*. The USAF successfully argued against such proposals on the grounds that the VFAX-F-14 was not a suitable replacement for the F-4E, nor could the F-4E be modified to meet the expected threat. The F-15 would include a ground-attack capability, as an option, after the air-superiority role was fulfilled.

On 23 December,

▼ **Two F15s of the 36th Tactical Fighter wing in flight over Germany.**

▲ An F15 *Strike Eagle* dual-role fighter drops a load of iron bombs while on a training mission over the desert.

1969 the bid for the new fighter was awarded to McDonnell Douglas by Secretary of the Air Force Robert G. Seamans Jr. The initial contract called for 20 aircraft: 10 single-seat F-15A, two twin-seat trainers (later designated F-15B), and eight Full Scale Development (FSD) aircraft with single seats. The eight FSD aircraft were closely matched to what would be the production aircraft.

The first F-15 rolled out of the hangar at St. Louis, Missouri, on 26 June, 1972 with all of the ceremony due to such an event. This aircraft was then taken apart and packed inside a C-5A Galaxy for shipment to Edwards Air Force Base, California. At Edwards it was reassembled, prepared for flight, and on 27 July, 1967 MCAIR's (McDonnell Douglas) chief pilot, Irving Burrows, made the maiden flight in the country's newest and hottest fighter plane.

In July 1971 the Secretary of Defense ordered the US Navy to consider the F-15 aeroplane as a lower-cost option to the costly F-14 fleet-defence fighter. Research by MCAIR indicated that a carrier version of the F-15N could be developed with an increased weight of 1,043 kg (2,300 lb). The Navy then did their own evaluation and concluded that by the time the aircraft was ready to employ the AIM-54 *Phoenix* missile it would be unacceptable in performance and cost. The study was finally concluded with a high/low mix being decided upon, and Northrop/McDonnell Douglas producing the navy F/A-18 *Hornet*.

CONTROL FORCES

Big, fast and powerful aeroplanes require big, fast and powerful control devices. This plane is controlled through a hydromechanical system for basic control surface deflections, and a Control Augmentation System that operates as a separate fly-by-wire system in addition to the basic one. Throughout flight testing, the control forces required by the pilot to safely and easily control the plane were worked out. Control forces around neutral are reported to be comfortable at all airspeeds and 6g manoeuvres can be flown with one hand. Crosswinds of 25 to 30 knots and a crab angle of up to 12 degrees are acceptable during landing. The pilot holds the nose up to 12 degrees and uses aerodynamic control to steer until the nose wheel touches down at about 80 knots, when nose wheel steering takes over.

ARMAMENT

The Eagle is equipped with the standard USAF General Electric M-61 Vulcan 20-mm cannon. The gun is mounted in the right wing root and the ammunition drum, holding 940 rounds, is mounted in the fuselage centreline. A dual chute carries the linkless rounds to the gun and the spent cases back to the drum. A special ground support system is used to reload the drum and remove the spent cases. Rate of fire is about 6,000 rounds per minute, or less than 10 seconds of actual cannon fire.

Although the F-15 Eagle carries the 20-mm cannon, missiles are still considered to be the primary air-to-air weapon. The AIM-7F *Sparrow* is the prime beyond-visual-range weapon, and for shorter ranges the *Eagle* carries the AIM-9 *Sidewinder*. The AIM-120 Advanced Medium Range Air to Air Missile (AMRAAM) under development by Hughes has been test fired from the F-15, and is expected to be used in future.

The newer version of the *Eagle*, called the *Strike Eagle*, is capable of carrying over 10,886 kg (24,000 lb) of external weapons, including anti-radiation missiles, *Maverick* "TV"-guided missiles, and all types of bombs. The bomb load can include the 907-kg (2,000-lb) Mk 82 laser-guided weapon. The MER-200 (BRU-26A/A) multiple ejection bomb rack allows a very flexible load to be carried by this ground-attack version of the *Eagle*.

PERFORMANCE

The F-15 is fitted with two Pratt and Whitney F-100 afterburning turbofan engines. The engine is rated at 14,420 lb of thrust at full military power without afterburner. With afterburning the engine develops almost 24,000 lb of thrust. The thrust-to-weight ratio is such that an *Eagle* will accelerate through Mach 1 while in a vertical climb, and has a maximum

▼ **An F-15 dual-role fighter armed with Sidewinders and iron bombs flies above the Arizona desert.**

▲ **The F-15E's controls are tested in the flight simulation facility at McDonnell Douglas. All F-15Es have a rear cockpit for a weapons system operator. On four cathode ray tubes, the operator can display information from a wide variety of aircraft and weapon systems.**

speed of 2,700 km/h (1,678 mph) at 47,200 ft altitude. This also means that the F-15 can climb over 7,000 ft while matching the tightest turn an F-4E is capable of making. A number of improved engines are under development by Pratt and Whitney as well as General Electric, and performance will undeniably improve in the future.

The electronics systems aboard the *Eagle* are state of the art and outclass most avionics in other aircraft. The Heads Up Display (HUD) presents all necessary navigation and attack information directly in front of the pilot's view. Additionally, much of the flight information and sensor information is controlled through an IBM on-board computer and presented to the pilot on a cathode ray tube (CRT) on the instrument panel. Navigation is through a Litton ASN-109 inertial navigation system as well as a full range of civilian-type radio navigation aids such as TACAN, ADF and ILS. Controls for all weapons are located on the throttles and control stick for ease of use. The Hughes APG-63 multi-mode, pulse-Doppler radar gives the pilot a powerful look-down ability as well as almost 160 km (100 miles) of view. This radar has been called the heart of the F-15.

One of the most interesting uses of an F-15 to date was to carry an anti-satellite (ASAT) missile to high altitude and high speed for launch. The ASAT missile was a 1,225-kg (2,700-lb) weapon measuring 543 cm (17 ft 9¾ in) long and 50 cm (19¾ in) wide. The missile was carried to about 80,000 ft altitude for launch. At least two successful launches and intercepts were made. However, the programme was deemed to be in violation of the anti-satellite treaty and stopped by congress.

COMBAT OPERATION

As might be expected, Israel became the first country to use the F-15 in combat. In 1979 Israel engaged Syrian aircraft and it has been reported that at least 80 Syrian jet fighters were downed in air-to-air combat. During the recent Middle East conflict, the F-15 *Eagle* was the backbone of the attack forces led by the United States. The F-15 led the ground attack as well as maintaining air superiority over the battlefield. Kuwaiti pilots in F-15s were among the first to shoot down Iraqi jet warplanes that were trying to escape to Iran. The premier American fighter has proven itself to be all that it was hoped it would become. None has been

▲ The US Air Force/McDonnell Douglas F-15 Short Takeoff and Landing Maneuver Technology Demonstrator (S/MTD) flew for the first time on May 10, 1989, with thrust-vectoring, thrust-reversing engine nozzles designed and manufacturerd by Pratt & Whitney. The thrust-vectoring nozzles are used on late model F-15s and the F-22 Advanced Tactical Fighter.

SPECIFICATION	
Wingspan:	1,304.93 cm (42 ft 9¾ in)
Length:	1,943.1 cm (63 ft 9 in)
Height:	562.61 cm (18 ft 5½ in)
Maximum take-off weight:	30,844.8 kg (68,000 lb)
Engines:	Two Pratt and Whitney F100-PW-100 turbofans
Engine Thrust:	24,000 lb with afterburner
Maximum Speed above 42,000 feet:	Mach 2.5+
Maximum Range (unrefuelled):	5,745.2 km (3,570 miles)
Service Ceiling:	60,000 ft

▲ The F-15 S/MTD research craft shown in a cut-away view. Layout is very similar to the F-15E.

reported lost in air-to-air combat, and the *Eagle* has a reported kill of over 100 enemy aircraft.

The future of the F-15 *Eagle* is assured into the 21st century with the latest model, the F-15E. Engine upgrades are continually being developed by Pratt and Whitley and General Electric for greater reliability and more thrust. The weapons load and combat capability are being expanded to include advanced missiles and massive bomb loads, forward-looking infra-red laser pods and long-range ground-mapping radar. Weapons are delivered with a greater accuracy than that achieved by A-7D *Corsair II*, F-4E *Phantom* and F-111E/F aircraft that were designed specifically for the ground-attack role. Other roles, such as tactical reconnaissance and electronic/radar suppression (Wild Weasel), have been considered and will most likely become common for the versatile *Eagle*.

GENERAL DYNAMICS F-16 FIGHTING FALCON

Aircraft development from the P-51 *Mustang* of World War II to the F-15 *Eagle* involved an ever-increasing level of power, size and cost. Each new aircraft had to be bigger and better, and therefore cost more. This process led the USAF to the requirement for a lightweight, low-cost and highly manoeuvrable Mach 2 fighter to complement the heavy, high-cost and highly manoeuvrable F-15 *Eagle*. The NATO nations were also looking for a replacement air-superiority fighter for the Lockheed F-104 *Starfighter*. The new lightweight fighter was designed for that role. To make the aircraft more attractive to the NATO allies it could be produced jointly in the NATO countries.

Major John Boyd's theory of "energy manoeuvrability" was followed during the development of the F-15 fighter, but when it was applied to the F-16 it caused opposition. The concept and theory were counter to the traditional thinking of many people, and were thought to be a threat to the F-15 *Eagle* programme. Major Boyd was able to push through the concept while working for the Air Force Prototype Study Group. Also, to reduce the ever-increasing cost of aircraft development, the Deputy Defense Secretary, David A. Packard, was in favour of prototype aircraft competing in a fly-off. As a result the YF-16A and YF-17A aircraft came into existence.

Five companies responded to the USAF request for proposals for the new fighter, with General Dynamics (YF-16) and Northrop (YF-17) selected to produce prototypes. The two prototypes flew against each other and on 13 April, 1972 the YF-16 was selected for production.

General Dynamics' (GD) design team exceeded USAF specifications in many areas. For example, the USAF called for a load factor of 7.33g with 80 per cent fuel, and GD increased this figure to 9g with a full internal fuel load. The aircraft was also made large enough to use heavier and larger avionics than the specifications called for. The fuel tanks were arranged so that the aircraft uses external fuel

▼ **A US Navy F16N model *Fighting Falcon* waits at rest on a concrete apron.**

on the flight to the combat area, and internal fuel during combat and for the return to base. Also, the engine is common to the F-15 *Eagle*, the Pratt and Whitney F-100, with 25,000 lb thrust.

Twenty-one months after the contract was awarded to General Dynamics, the first prototype was rolled out and welcomed to the USAF. This aircraft was then shipped inside a C-5A to Edwards Air Force Base for flight testing. What was to have been the first high-speed taxi run inadvertently became an unofficial flight when control roll oscillations occurred. The test pilot, Phil Oestricher, had allowed the speed to reach 241.4 km/h (150 mph) and decided to lift the aircraft off in order to solve the control problem. A short flight occurred followed by a smooth landing. The problem was solved by reducing the gain of the electric fly-by-wire system by 50 per cent while the aircraft is on the ground, then increasing it to full value automatically when the aircraft lifts off.

On only the third official flight the fighter was taken to supersonic speed, Mach 1.2, for five minutes. Manoeuvres at up to 5g were performed during this supersonic flight time. The performance of the YF-16 (and the YF-17) was so good that before the second YF-16 had flown, Defense Secretary James R. Schlesinger had decided that the winning contender would be developed into an operational type designated Air Combat Fighter (ACF). During test flights against fighter aircraft it was shown that the YF-16 outclassed the Soviet MiG-21, and may possibly outclass the newer MiG-29. On 13 January, 1975 the YF-16 was selected as the winning aeroplane over the Northrop YF-17.

The USAF had considered ordering 650 of the new aircraft and the US Navy wanted 800. Also, NATO nations were intending to order and build a standard NATO fighter, and wanted the selection decision made quickly. The US Navy dropped out of the programme when they decided there was not enough information to make a decision by January 1975. The Navy continued to test both aircraft, but did not purchase either. The F-16 was selected by NATO as a standard fighter on 2 June, 1975. Production of the first F-16 started in the same month it was selected as the winning lightweight fighter, and production continues to the present time.

ARMAMENT

Armament for the F-16 is the standard USAF M61A1 20 mm Vulcan six-barrel cannon with 500 rounds of Linkless ammunition stored in a drum in the centre of the fuselage. Wing-tip stations carry the AIM-9

▼ **An armed F-16 flies low on a training flight in Germany, a fairy-tale castle rising out of the forest in the background.**

HI-TECH PLANES

▲ **The pilot of an F-16** has an excellent all-round view from his position high in the clear, one-piece canopy; the pilot turning his head is the only large body movement required to fly the F-16.

Sidewinder missile. The remaining nine pylons can carry a bewildering variety of bombs and missiles, including the 907-kg (2,000-lb) guided bomb, *Maverick*, *Sparrow* and the advanced Hughes AIM-120 ASRAAM missile. Up to 25 of the Mk82 227-kg (500-lb) bombs can be carried.

PERFORMANCE AND HANDLING

The pilot in an F-16 sits at a 30-degree reclined angle and has a side-arm control stick under a completely clear one-piece canopy, giving the illusion of riding on top of a telegraph pole. After releasing the brakes and applying full power, the fighter quickly picks up speed, rotates at around 125 knots and lifts off at 140 knots. Bring the nose up to a 60-degree climb and the pilot's body is horizontal. The F-16 will climb and accelerate as far as you like,

GENERAL DYNAMICS F-16 FIGHTING FALCON

and the fighter will continue to accelerate even in a vertical climb.

For control, only a few millimetres of stick movement and 12 mm (½ in) of rudder movement are required, so only the pilot's head needs room to move. The clear one-piece canopy gives a splendid view in all directions. The Heads Up Display (HUD) acts as a windscreen in the event of loss of the canopy. The turn rate is 20 degrees per second – the same as an F-14 *Tomcat* and F-20 *Tigershark*, and slightly less than the F/A-18 *Hornet*.

During the Gulf War the F-16 *Fighting Falcon* performed yeoman duty with the USAF Tactical Air Command. Bombing missions were conducted continuously from the opening air campaign to the end of the war. The lightweight fighter proved it was everything except a lightweight.

▼ **A *Fighting Falcon* with gear down, ready to land.**

FIRST COMBAT

On 2 July, 1980 the first F-16s were delivered to Israel, after which they continued to receive four planes a month. These aircraft contained modified hardware and computer software in order to meet Israeli needs. Only 14 months later the fighters carried out the bombing raid on the Osirak nuclear reactor under construction near Bagdad, Iraq. The F-16 was chosen because of its long range, and yet the fighter had been designed as a short-range aircraft. According to available reports eight F-16s equipped as bombers and six F-15 *Eagles* as top cover conducted the raid. Tactical surprise was achieved at 6.00 am on a Sunday morning, and there was only light anti-aircraft fire. No SAMS or interceptors were seen. The F-16s dropped either precision guided bombs or, depending on which report you read, unguided iron bombs and within minutes the reactor was badly damaged by multiple direct hits. The second wave of four F-16 did not bomb because of the damage done by the first wave. All aircraft returned to base without damage.

In 1982 the F-16 *Fighting Falcon* was again in air combat, this time over the Bekaa valley in Lebanon against the Syrian Air Force. The Syrians were equipped with Soviet planes, including the MiG-21, MiG-23 and SU-22. F-16s were credited with shooting down 44 Syrian MiGs and the F-15 *Eagle* was credited with 40 MiGs. A total of up to 92 Syrian fighters were shot down.

SPECIFICATION

Wingspan:	944.88 cm (31 ft)
Length:	1,503.67 cm (49 ft 4 in)
Height:	509.27 cm (16 ft 8½ in)
Maximum weight:	19,187.28 kg (42,300 lb)
Engine:	One Pratt and Whitney F-100
Engine Upgrade:	One GE F-110-GE-100 turbofan or one Pratt & Whitney F-100-PE-220
Engine Thrust:	Up to 29,000 lb
Maximum Speed:	Mach 2+
Service Ceiling:	50,000 ft

▶ An F-16 in a vertical climb.

MIGs... AN OVERVIEW

MIG! The name may not strike terror into the hearts of people everywhere, but the name is known throughout the world as one of what was the Soviet Unions' great warplanes. Every boy in the United States and Western Europe that plays with paper aeroplanes knows just what a MiG is and where it comes from. He may not know *which* MiG, but he knows *a* MiG.

There should be no doubt in any person's mind that when someone talks about a MiG they are talking about a good military aeroplane. Each MiG was designed for a specific role, and the plane fulfills that role in a manner that is satisfactory to the military leaders who needed the plane in the first place. While a MiG may not be as multi-purpose as a Western counterpart, or as pilot-oriented, it serves the designated combat mission assigned to it with great zeal.

The name MiG (or MIG) is an abbreviation for the Soviet airplane design establishment named after its principal design team: Artem Mikoyan and Mikhail Guryevich. This team came together during World War II (in Soviet history texts, The Great Patriotic War) during a time of great need for weapons of all types. Mr Mikoyan directed the organization from age 34 until his death in 1970. The first aeroplane from the group was the MiG-1, a high-altitude fighter. The first jet was the MiG-9, followed by the hugely successful MiG-15. The world's first operational supersonic fighter was also a MiG, the MiG-19, which was used with success against American air forces during the Vietnam War.

In reaction to Western planes like the F-104 and British *Lightning*, the MiG-21 flew into aviation history during the mid-50s, and is still in use in several countries in the 1990s. The MiG-21 has gone through many modifications and has formed the basis for some of the more advanced aeroplanes produced later. Also, the MiG-21 has been built in quantities challenged only by the later MiG-23/27 and the American F-4 *Phantom II*. Over 5,000 of each of these aircraft have been built, and over 8,000 MiG-21s.

In the Soviet Union the driving force for design and production of a weapon system was an assessment of the threat they believed faced the country. In response to the perceived threat a countermeasure was developed and put into service. The Soviets did not normally develop technology first, and then find a fuse for it as is somewhat the case in the West. A Western nation has traditionally pushed the limits of technology to incorporate it into a new system, whereas the Soviets developed the technology as needed. This has sometimes caused the delay of some modern equipment being fielded by the Soviets, but not for any extended period of time.

A case in point is the ability of a fighter/interceptor to "Look down, shoot down" during the intercepting of hostile planes or cruise missiles. Only after the USAF developed the low-level penetration B-1 bomber did the Soviet Union produce and field a radar with this capability. The Soviet response to the F-15, F-16 mix was the Su-27 and MiG-29. The US has the ability to over-react to Soviet threats as well as anyone, and the American response to the MiG-25 was near hysteria.

▲ A MiG-21 in flight.

MIG-25 FOXBAT

The MiG-25 was a costly fighter for the US, as well as the Soviet Union. Because of the near hysteria in USAF circles about the capability of this fighter/interceptor, the USAF forced the F-15 programme into capabilities that were not needed. This drove up the cost, size and complexities of the F-15 to new heights for a weapon system. However, the ability of the F-15 today is almost beyond being equalled.

In the early 1960s the USA considered the manned bomber to be one of the three legs of nuclear deterrence. The requirements for the manned bomber were greater than the ability of the USAF B-58 *Hustler*, and the next generation bomber was under development. This aircraft was designated the XB-70 and was a Mach 3, high-altitude intercontinental bomber. The design would trap and ride its own shock wave for extra long supersonic flight at altitudes up to 70,000 ft.

The XB-70 went higher and faster than any Soviet interceptor could reach, and also beyond range of most of the air-defence missiles. In response to this threat to Soviet national security the Mikoyan-Gurevich design bureau produced the MiG-25 fighter/interceptor airplane. It was imperative that this new interceptor should also combat the USAF B-58 supersonic bomber. The MiG-25 sacrificed many capabilities to achieve such high speed and altitude, but we should remember that the goal was in fact reached; the aircraft would fly at 3,220 km/h (2,000 mph) at 80,000 ft carrying air-to-air missiles to fight with.

The MiG-25 is built with a large percentage of steel instead of aluminium. Titanium skin is used in places where heat is a problem and on all leading edges. Titanium is not a major component of the plane as it is in the USAF SR-71 reconnaissance plane. The MiG is not subject to fuel leakage on the ground either. The Soviets developed a process to continuously weld nickel steel to produce leak-proof fuel tanks. While this does reduce the internal fuel that can be carried, the reduced range was not critical to the plane's use.

ENGINES

The engines that power this aircraft are Tumansky R-31 turbojets with huge afterburner sections. This engine gulps huge quantities of air but produces only a low-pressure output. The large amount of high-oxygen content air allows the afterburner sec-

▼ **A MiG-25 taxis towards the runway. The length of the engines allows for the huge afterburners.**

tion to generate most of the thrust produced by the engine. The plane also carries 520 kg (1,000 lb) of methanol/water mixture to inject into the incoming air to cool it. This allows increased thrust while keeping the engine temperature within limits.

The R-31 engine develops its power only in high-speed flight. To illustrate this, consider that it develops only 12% more static thrust than an F-15A's engine, yet the aircraft is 60% faster than an F-15A. The MiG-25 is not designed to compete with the F-15, it is designed to fly high and fast, and to carry large anti-aircraft guided missiles in a bomber interception role.

A digression about the alcohol used in the plane is reported by Lt. Viktor Belenko in the book "MiG Pilot". Lt. Belenko stated that a large percentage of the alcohol was consumed by the station personnel.

One of the reasons the USAF and NATO believed the exaggerated performance of the MiG-25 was related to where the plane was stationed in Europe. The MiGs were stationed in the same location in Poland from which long-range, Mach 2.8 reconnaissance drones were stationed and operated. Western observers tracked the drones at 90,000 ft, flying at Mach 2.8, for a radius of operations exceeding 1,600 km (1,000 miles), and thought they were watching MiG-25 flights. The myths and legends about the MiG-25 continued until Lt. Viktor Belenko defected and landed his plane at Hakodate, Japan.

▼ **A MiG-25 waits on the tarmac to be towed. The large air intakes gulp great quantities of air as the aircraft flies.**

▲ **A MiG-25 Mach 3 interceptor in flight carrying a large air-to-air missile.**

WEAPONS

The MiG-25 is equipped with one of the most powerful radar search units ever to be mounted in a fighter. The purpose of this power is to "burn through" the electronic jamming given off by enemy bombers and guide a missile to interception. To give the missile the best chance of success required a large warhead of about 130 kg (285 lb) of explosive. To carry the warhead required a large engine, and the result is the largest air-to-air missile in the world, the AA-6 *Acid*. This missile is slightly larger than the ground-launched *Hawk* surface-to-air missile. Its effectiveness has never been tested in combat, but it is reported to be slow and not very effective against fast-moving targets.

Soviet military pilots have never been as well trained, or trusted, as Western pilots are. One consequence of this philosophy is how Soviet interception operations take place.

COMBAT ROLE

A Soviet MiG-25 is flown primarily by a ground intercept operator, and weapons can be fired by that same operator. The ground controller commands the autopilot controls. The interceptor works like a surface-to-air missile (SAM) with the ability to make multiple attack passes at a target. The short range of the interceptor keeps it tied to nearby ground bases. Beyond visual range (BVR) attacks are not greatly needed, and with the powerful short-range search radar the large air-to-air (AA) missile has a good chance of being successful. In the event that radar cannot get a good target position, the MiG-25 is also equipped with passive infra-red sensing equipment.

After the MiG-25 was taken apart in Japan and all of its secrets revealed, the Soviet military allowed it to be exported to friends in other nations. Egypt took delivery of several, and Col. Moamar al Gadhafi of Libya got a few. In Egypt the MiG-25 thumbed its nose at Israel and at least once one of the reconnaissance planes was tracked at Mach 3.2 while over the Sinai Peninsula.

The fact that the engines would be wrecked at that power setting is an accepted fact for the aircraft. Soviet planners know the life expectancy is short, and replacements are available. The engine is designed for low maintenance during its life, and it is then returned to the factory for overhaul. This may be different from the Western way, but it works well for them.

▼ The huge afterburners of what is essentially a modified cruise missile engine glow as a MiG-25 accelerates to take off.

In 1982 the Israeli Defence Force managed to destroy two MiG-25s in air-to-air combat. These were Syrian jets over Lebanon. The method of operation has not been published, but it is thought to have been carried out by planned intercept and pop-up missile attack.

Most of the MiG-25 fighters in service today have been converted to *Foxbat-E* specifications. They now carry the same radar as the MiG-23 and the improved IR search-and-track system. The present engines (if equipped with them) are capable of 31,000 lb of thrust. The MiG-25 is over 25 years old, and still a very dangerous threat to USAF command-and-control craft. If it were to be built today we would call it the MiG-31. More about that later.

SPECIFICATION	
Wingspan:	1,394.46 cm (45 ft 9 in)
Length:	2,382.52 cm (78 ft 2 in)
Height:	606.14 cm (20 ft 1 in)
Weight, maximum:	35,834.4 kg (79,000 lb)
Engine Thrust:	27,000 lb
Maximum Speed above 36,000 ft:	Mach 3.2
Maximum Range:	Unknown
Combat Radius:	1,448.4 km (900 miles)
Service Ceiling:	80,000 ft

MIG-23 FLOGGER

During the early 1960s a replacement craft for the MiG-21 was under development in the Mikoyan/Guryevich design bureau. This aircraft was intended to cure many of the design deficiencies of the previous model, and provide a multi-role aircraft for the Soviet Aviation Armies. The new plane was intended to be faster in level flight, climb and accelerate faster, and have a greater range. (The Soviet need for range is not as important to design as it is in the USA). The size and cost of the new plane was to be kept as low as possible and performance could be traded for ease of production.

The selection of a VG (variable geometry) wing was probably the best solution to the requirements laid down at the time. The only other solution considered was an aeroplane with two smaller "lift jets" in addition to the main engine. While it may not sound like such a good idea, the lift-jet version was flown for some time and does operate satisfactorily. However, the VG wing gives the best of several worlds to the fighter, and that is what was selected.

A VG wing allows a lower takeoff and landing speed with the wings spread, and a much higher top speed with the wings swept back. The smaller area at full sweep also gives a smoother flight at high speed and low level. However, when the wing is swept back other problems occur such as pitch stability increasing and the position of the horizontal tail surfaces becoming critical. Increased pitch stability cannot be allowed to become so great that control of the aircraft is endangered. The point on the wingspan where the movable portion begins is a compromise between cost, performance and weight. On the MiG-23 the sweep point was arrived at by that process of compromise, but did not reduce the ability of the aeroplane to perform its mission.

ENGINES

The engine selection for the MiG-23 was made based on the plane's role. The aircraft was not expected to have a sustained high Mach speed, nor was it expected to have to loiter over the battlefield for any extended time. The range requirement was not so great that specific fuel consumption was a

▼ **A MiG-23MF awaits its pilot and navigator, the two canopies open. The variable geometry wings are in the forward position.**

▲ **A MiG-23 cruises against an evening sky.** Although the engines were not designed for sustained supersonic flight, the aircraft can maintain over Mach 2.

critical factor. If both turbofan and turbojet engines were considered, then the easier engine to develop won. The engine selected was the Tumansky R-27 turbojet. It is similar to the USJ-79, but has about 25% more thrust.

WEAPONS

By the early 1970s the MiG-23 was in operation with the Soviet military units. It fills the role of supersonic fighter as well as ground-attack aircraft. An internal cannon was designed into it and a twin-barrel cannon pod is sometimes carried. Missile armament consists of short range IR homing missiles (R-60, AA-8 "Aphid") and the R-23 BVR (Beyond Visual Range), AA-7 "Apex". The R-60 is a short-range, high manoeuvrability missile and can be equipped with either infra-red or semi-active radar guidance.

The radar carried on the MiG-23 is similar to the type used in the F-4 *Phantom*. It has the ability to look down and see a target, but cannot guide a missile to that target. It has been suggested that the radar, code name "High Lark" was developed from US units recovered in Vietnam.

The Western world and NATO began to understand the MiG-23 in about 1973 when the plane began showing up in great numbers throughout the Soviet sphere. By 1975 there were new versions of the MiG in operational units and production was estimated at somewhere around 500 units a year. The greatest success of the MiG-23 was that it could be produced in such huge numbers, and still be an outstanding aeroplane. The USA was forced to re-evaluate Soviet ability in light of this information.

A major change of role, without significant changes to the aircraft, brought about the MiG-27 *Flogger D* variant. It was decided that a dedicated ground-attack version would be developed from the existing airframe. While retaining the VG wing and systems used for ground attack, the requirements and capability of Mach 2+ flight were removed. The result was a cheaper, heavier load carrying plane that could be manufactured in vast numbers.

A number of different items show up on the MiG-27 version. One is an increased wing cord that terminates in a prominent "claw" near the wing root. The wing addition gives much better load-carrying ability, while the claw causes an improved air flow and reduces the wing tip stall during high "g" operation. An unrated engine has been installed, the R-29 Tumansky, with 15% better thrust.

A six-barrel rotary cannon is installed in the righthand wing-glove area on some MiG-23s. This gun is completely exposed and can be traversed

◀ **A MiG-23 of the Czechoslovakian airforce.**

vertically by the pilot. The purpose of the elevation control is not fully understood. However, during one firing pass an automatic depression during the firing time would cause a much greater percentage of shells to land on a tank/sized target. The cannon is of the 23-mm type used by many Soviet weapons and fires about 5,000 rounds per minute.

The MiG-27 also has additional cockpit armour, thought to be titanium, bolted to the outside of the airframe. This provides a substantial increase in pilot protection during low-level operations without greatly adding to airframe weight. In line with most Soviet equipment, the MiG-27 can operate from fairly poor airstrips. The wheels are large low-pressure ones suitable to dirt-strip operations.

The weapons load of the MiG-23/27 is a mixture of missiles, bombs, air-to-ground rockets and larger guided air-to-ground bombs such as laser-guided munitions. The aircraft centre-line pylon and two wing-glove pylons are rated to carry 9,000-kg (2,200-lb) bombs. On the later version provisions are made to carry two large external fuel tanks on the outer wing. These tanks must be jettisoned before the wings can be swept, but they increase the range of the aircraft.

COMBAT

Observations, pictures and knowing about the performance of the MiG-23/27 leads military people to expect certain high standards of effectiveness from it. The MiGs were used in Afghanistan with satisfactory results, until the deployment of the US *Stinger* shoulder-launched anti-aircraft missile.

Whenever the MiG-23/27 has operated in a theatre in which hostile air forces were operating, the MiGs have come up short. It has proven to be no match for the US F-14 *Tomcat* over the waters off the coast of Lybia. The Israeli Air Forces shot down at least 35 of the MiGs in one week in June 1982. This aircraft is one of the backbone planes in the Soviet military and would probably fare much better in a conflict in Europe – as long as it did not run up against F-15 or F-16 fighters.

▼ A MiG-23ML, carrying a fuel pod, waits at a Czech airforce base.

SPECIFICATION

Wingspan:	
MINIMUM:	828.04 cm (27 ft 2 in)
MAXIMUM:	1,424.94 cm (46 ft 9 in)
Length:	2,023.72 cm (59 ft 10 in)
Height:	436.87 cm (14 ft 4 in)
Weight, max takeoff:	19,278 kg (42,500 lb)
Empty Weight:	11,340 kg (25,000 lb)
Engine:	One Tumansky R-29 turbojet
Engine Thrust:	17,500 lb
With afterburning:	25,300 lb
Maximum Speed:	Mach 2.35
Combat radius:	804.65 km (500 miles)
Service Ceiling:	61,000 ft

MIG-29 FULCRUM

The Soviet Union delayed introducing new fighter planes during the 1970s, but they did not delay the design process of maintaining a counter to new Western aircraft. The introduction of the USAF F-15 and F-16 in the 1970s brought about the later Soviet response in the form of the Su-27, MiG-29 and MiG-31 models. By delaying introduction for just a few years the Soviet design bureaux were able to produce planes that can confront the US planes on at least equal terms.

A second reason for the final design in the MiG-29 is the requirement to combat the NATO ability to fly at a very low altitude of about 75 m (250 ft) above the trees. This required a better radar than was available at the start of the design process. A pulse-Doppler radar for look-down, shoot-down requirement was developed to guide the semi-active radar-guided missile to the target.

Design criteria for this aircraft called for agility to match the USAF F-16's 9g constant turn rate. It is not known whether the MiG-29 will totally match this rate, but it is considered to be very close to this ability. The high-thrust engines required to meet this demand were also needed to handle the supersonic level-speed requirement of Mach 2.3.

▼ **The MiG-29 at rest. Note the doors covering the lower air intakes during ground operations.**

The external shape of the MiG-29 clearly shows that it descended from the MiG-25 series. Wingspan and sweep are like the MiG-25, as well as the dual vertical fins and air inlets. The cockpit canopy is designed for pilot visibility while accepting the small additional drag imposed. The tail and fins are cut off at an angle parallel to about one-third of the surface cord. This is done to reduce the possibility of flutter.

LARX

One prominent feature of the plan (top) view of the MiG-29 is the large size of the wing-root extension, called Larx. This highly-swept section of the wing gives a lot of flight benefits, but requires a great deal of research in getting the right decision for the aeroplane. The Larx generates a lot of lift at high angles of attack and caused destabilizing in the pitch axis. This reduces the amount of elevator control required to maintain the angle of attack, as well as reducing the wing loading. The Larx does not stall as the wing does at high angle of attack, but sheds a vortex over the wing that maintains airflow and reduces wing-tip stall.

WEAPONS

Weapons for the MiG-29 include up to six missiles, and two large cannons. One cannon is mounted on each side in the Larx. The amount of gun ammunition is not known at this time. The missiles

MiG-29 FULCRUM

▲ **A MiG-29 climbing shortly after takeoff during an airshow.**

include infrared (IR) seeking AA-8 "Aphid". A new 40-km (25-mile) range radar-guided missile, the AA-10, is also believed to be a main weapon. The AA-10 missile uses an active seeker in the terminal flight phase for beyond-visual-range engagement. A complete infra-red search and tracking system is installed, as well as a laser range-finder on some of the aircraft.

ENGINES

The MiG-29 is larger than the F-16 and about the same size as the F/A-18. Like the F-16, it is controlled by an active fly-by-wire (FBW) system. This is believed to be the first Soviet fighter to use the FBW system. The size also demanded two engines because no single engine available produced enough power to meet mission demands. The engines are set as far apart as practical, but not so far as to leave a flat fuselage section between them. All tail surfaces attach directly to the fuselage and not to an extension unit.

The inside structure has yet to be described in Western books, but is believed to be aluminium, steel and titanium. Some observers think that there may be some composite material, while others believe a larger percentage of titanium will be used.

▼ **A top view of the MiG-29 shows the wingroot extensions (or Larx). The resemblance to the MiG-25 series can be seen in the overall shape of the aircraft.**

▲ A MiG-29 banking as it turns.
It is thought that the aircraft's turning ability is similar to that of the US F-16.

SPECIFICATION	
Wingspan:	1,150 cm (37 ft 8¾ in)
Length:	1,777.18 cm (56 ft 8 in)
Height:	440.06 cm (14 ft 5¼ in)
Weight, maximum:	18,008 kg (39,700 lb)
Engines:	Two RD-33 Tumansky turbofans
Engine Thrust:	18,300 lb
Maximum Speed above 36,000 ft:	Mach 2.3
Range:	2,092 km (1,300 miles)
Service Ceiling:	56,000 ft

The MiG-29 is powered by a pair of Tumansky R-33D late-design engines. They are believed to be low-bypass turbofan engines, and would be the first fanjets in a production fighter in the Soviet Union. The engines each produce about 18,500 lb of dry thrust. The amount of thrust and the flight capability leads observers to believe that a ground-attack version will be produced. The only question about that is whether it will be done like the MiG-23/27, with a version with reduced air superiority capability. In either case, the MiG-29 could become a very good ground-attack craft, as well as being a good interceptor.

It is reported that a MiG-29 was flown into Turkey and landed by a defecting pilot. The Soviets immediately demanded the return of their aircraft. It was a coincidence that the defence minister of Turkey was in Moscow at the same time. The government and military of Turkey gladly gave the plane back to the USSR – after it was taken apart. The pilot (first name Alex) is reportedly sequestered in the USA somewhere, writing a book!

◀ A ground view of the back of a Solviet MiG-29.

MIG-31 FOXHOUND

The MiG-31, NATO code name *Foxhound*, is undoubtedly the world's premier interceptor. Although not as fast in level flight as the MiG-25, it is a superior interceptor, and in a class by itself in world aviation.

Development of this fighter was started at around the same time as discussion about the American B-1 bomber requirement, in 1960. In 1965 the design process was initiated on the B-1, and the Soviet response was development of the MiG-31. In the Soviet view, this was a necessary response to a clear and present danger to the USSR in the form of a new USAF low-level penetration bomber, the B-1.

The B-1 bomber was much more than just a weapons threat. The entire structure of the air defence system in the Soviet Union was threatened. The possession of a large number of airfields and radar ground control of short-ranged interceptors would be useless against the B-1, because as soon as the aircraft descended below the ground radar coverage all Soviet control would be lost. The B-1 bomber would have been able to overfly most of the USSR at very low altitude, and been mostly immune to hostile intercept.

With a change in the basic arrangement of Soviet air defence, the airframe requirements of the new interceptor were considered. The older MiG-25 external shape was retained because it is a superb supersonic aircraft. The maximum level speed was reduced to Mach 2.4, enabling more efficient engines to be used. Only necessary changes to the forward section were made, with the addition of a rear cockpit for a weapons/systems operator. The MiG-31 is a totally new airplane, only the outside shape of the earlier MiG-25 is retained. Also, the Soviet Union has had 25 years of development of titanium processing to use in the new version.

AVIONICS

Because the interceptor has to be able to find a target in low-level flight, an upgraded look-down, shoot-down radar system was installed. This is pulse-Doppler system of about the same capability as the one on the F/A-18 *Hornet*. The two-man crew, large radar unit, and the size of the missiles carried

▼ **A rear view of a MiG-31 on the ground at the Le Bourget air show. Its engine exhausts are covered and various external armaments are on the ground around it.**

▲ **A MiG-31 on the ground at an airshow. The basic shape of the MiG-25 is retained.**

drove the size of this aircraft to about the weight of the F-111A. The MiG-31 carries a large internal multi-barrel cannon mounted in the lower fuselage. This large aircraft's empty weight is about equal to the F-15's maximum takeoff weight.

An improved AA-9 large air-to-air radar guided missile is the primary weapon. This combination has been recorded making an intercept of supersonic drones flying above 70,000 ft. The same missile is capable of intercepting very low-level targets. Like the *Phoenix* system, multiple interceptions can be carried out at the same time. The missile capability is considered to be about the same as the *Phoenix* carried by the US Navy's F-14 *Tomcat*.

ENGINES

The engines installed in this MiG are believed to be upgraded Tumansky engines in the 22,000 lb dry thrust class. Maximum thrust is about 32,000 lb. The body is longer than the MiG-25, and a larger quantity of fuel is carried internally. Large fuel tanks can be fitted to the wing, displacing two of the large missiles. The reduced maximum speed allows more efficient engines, and gives it a longer range.

COMBAT

The MiG-31 is teamed with the "Mainstay" AEW&C (Airborne Early Warning and Control) aircraft which may match the ability to control interceptors of the USAF E-3 AWAC. This gives the Soviets the ability to cover a large portion of the USSR and defend against a low-level penetration threat. The high supersonic capability combined with the reported 1,287-km (800-mile) range gives the Soviet Air Force the ability to attack incoming deep interdiction aircraft such as the USAF F-15E and the NATO *Tornado*. Before the introduction of the MiG-31, these aircraft were reasonably safe at low-level flight. A significant threat posed by the MiG-31 is its ability to attack Western command-and-control aircraft, or stand-off reconnaissance aircraft, with a very short warning time. Operating at over 70,000 ft altitude and Mach 2.4, the Mig-31 will be difficult for Western fighters to intercept or deter from making an assault.

The MiG-31 is considered to be the foremost interceptor in the world today. The airframe is optimized for supersonic speed, and is not compromised by expecting it to perform dog fights. The MiG-31 is designed, built and deployed to intercept and attack incoming hostile aircraft and cruise missiles. With the advent of the USAF *Stealth Bomber*, the planners of future aircraft to be produced by what was the Soviet military establishment will have to continue to improve the breed to have an effective interceptor.

▶ **A MiG-31 in flight.**

SPECIFICATION	
WINGSPAN:	1,430.66 cm (46 ft 11¼ in)
LENGTH:	2,150.11 cm (70 ft 6½ in)
HEIGHT:	561.34 cm (18 ft 5 in)
WEIGHT:	
MAXIMUM TAKE-OFF:	41,152.86 kg (90,725 lb)
EMPTY:	Not available
ENGINES:	Two Tumansky turbojets
ENGINE THRUST:	22,000/32,000 lb)
MAXIMUM SPEED:	Mach 2.4
COMBAT RADIUS:	2,092 km (1,300 miles)
SERVICE CEILING:	75,000 ft

SU-27 FLANKER

The newest Soviet fighter is the Sukhoi Su-27 *Flanker*. This aircraft has been optimized for the air-superiority role, and is assumed to be a match for the USAF F-15 fighter. The West got its first look at this sleek and powerful plane at the 1989 Paris Air Show where it demonstrated outstanding flight manoeuvrability. One sequence demonstrated the ability to come to a complete stop in a vertical climb, slide down for a short distance, then recover to normal flight. A second view was of the aircraft at an extreme angle of attack (90°+), and able to recover to level flight. Clearly, this is a very manoeuvrable fighter.

While the MiG-29 and the Su-27 appear to share the same shape, they are two very different aircraft. The Su-27 is a much larger plane, with a considerably greater weapons load. It also can be refuelled in flight, so the range of the fighter is limited by the pilot's endurance. The long range of 4,023 km (2,500 miles) on internal fuel means that this aircraft can reach the United Kingdom from Soviet bases in Eastern Europe. This is the first new long-range fighter from the Soviet Union and reflects the change in air defence policy in that country.

▼ **An SU-27 makes a low pass with the big air brake deployed.**

The mission of the Su-27 is clearly to be an all-weather air-superiority and armada-defence aircraft. A two-man crew, a load capacity of ten air-to-air missiles, and a 30-mm internal cannon makes the Su-27 well armed to engage in air combat. For maximum flight control an advanced fly-by-wire (FBW) system is used. Leading-edge slats and trailing-edge flaps are controlled by a computer during flight to maximize combat manoeuvrability and control. During takeoff and landing the slats and flaps are controlled directly by the pilot. All of these systems should also enhance control for carrier operations.

WEAPONS AND AVIONICS

A powerful pulse-Doppler radar fills the nose cone and is supplemented with laser ranging units. A large IR sensing unit is mounted on the nose just forward of the canopy. All the sensing units feed their information into an integrated fire-control unit, and allow the pilot to control the weapons through a helmet-mounted sight and a heads-up display. The pulse-Doppler radar gives the fighter a look-down, shoot-down capability.

The Su-27 *Flanker* can carry up to ten missiles. This includes two of the AA-10 "Alamo" or AA-9 "Amos", or four of the AA-8 Aphids or AA-11 "Archers". Missiles for all types

▲ A bottom view of the large SU-27 *Flanker* air-superiority fighter.

of air combat are available, including long-range, low-level target, and close-in air superiority fighting. The amount of ammunition that the Su-27 carries for the 30-mm cannon is not known.

A navy version was designed for service on board the new Soviet carriers. This model has reinforced landing gear with two nose wheels, an arresting hook and catapult launch capability. This model, the Su-27B2, does not have the underside air-inlet doors necessary for the ground-based type. It also has small canards on the forward fuselage for better low-speed control, necessary for a carrier approach. The wing panels fold up for carrier storage. Not much is known about this model.

The Su-27 is manufactured in the Soviet plant at Komsomolsy, and is being delivered to air defence units in quantity. Because of the large size, complexity and cost, the CIS countries are not expected to build Su-27s in large quantities for themselves. If it turns out to be as good a plane as some Western observers believe it is, however, then very large numbers of Su-27s could be expected to show up around the world.

▼ An SU-27 taxis by, showing its sleek shape and the exhausts of its powerful engines.

HI-TECH PLANES

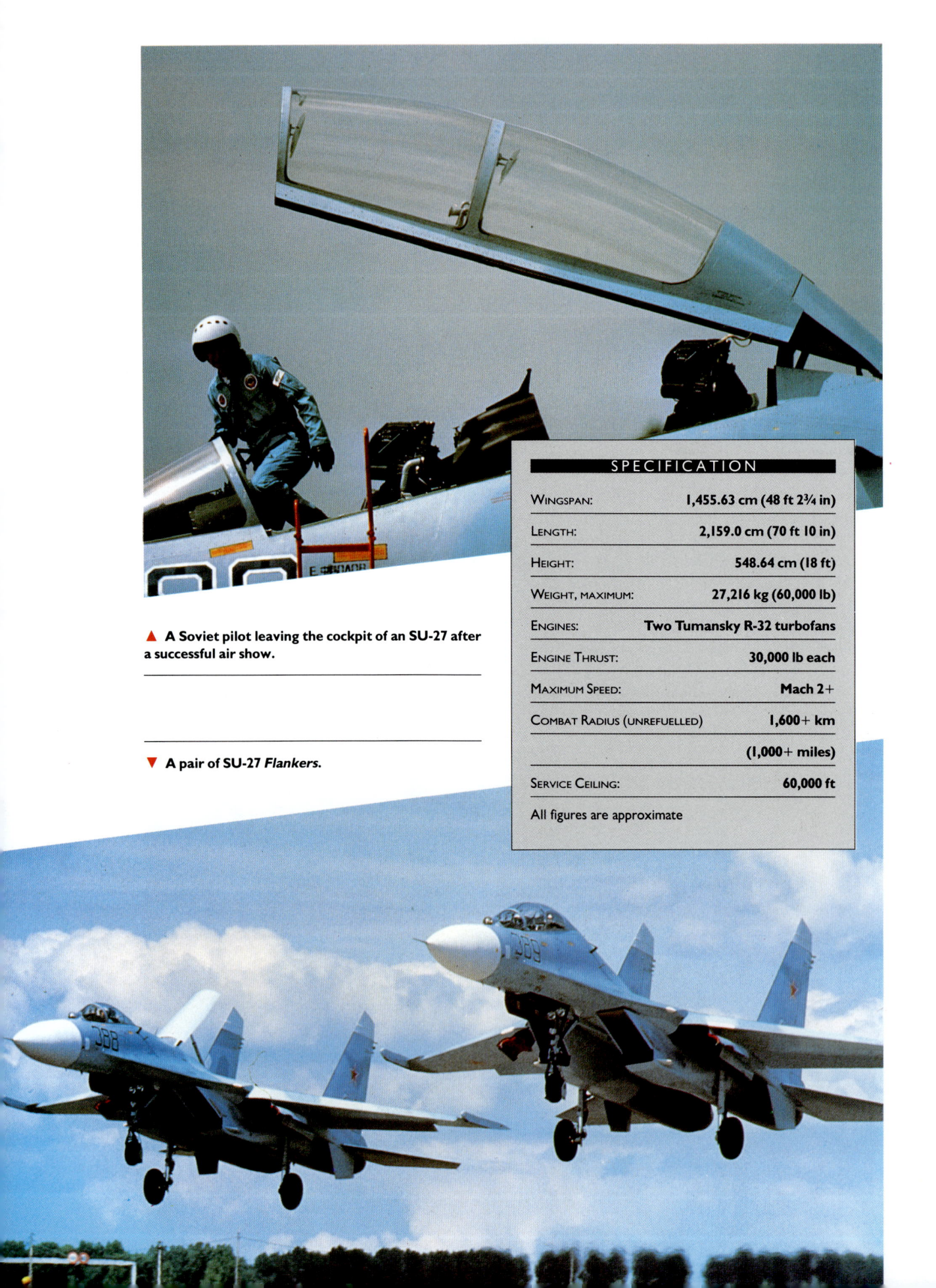

▲ **A Soviet pilot leaving the cockpit of an SU-27 after a successful air show.**

▼ **A pair of SU-27 *Flankers*.**

SPECIFICATION	
WINGSPAN:	1,455.63 cm (48 ft 2¾ in)
LENGTH:	2,159.0 cm (70 ft 10 in)
HEIGHT:	548.64 cm (18 ft)
WEIGHT, MAXIMUM:	27,216 kg (60,000 lb)
ENGINES:	Two Tumansky R-32 turbofans
ENGINE THRUST:	30,000 lb each
MAXIMUM SPEED:	Mach 2+
COMBAT RADIUS (UNREFUELLED)	1,600+ km
	(1,000+ miles)
SERVICE CEILING:	60,000 ft

All figures are approximate

B-1B BOMBER

The B-1 bomber has been given many unfavourable, as well as favourable, accolades. The truth is, most of them are based on fact. The B-1 was the most talked about and designed aeroplane in the USAF when it was finally produced. It was cancelled by one president, and restarted by the succeeding president, albeit in a different form for a different perceived mission.

In 1960 a series of discussions was started concerning the future manned bomber needs of the United States. These discussions and planning sessions lasted five years and culminated in the decision to design and produce an advanced bomber. The new bomber would not have the capability of the Mach 3 XB-70. It would not fly as high, nor would it be as fast at only Mach 2.0. A major reason for the decision was the belief that "higher and faster" was no longer desirable because low, subsonic penetration was now possible. Also, a manned bomber would force the Soviet Union to divert large resources to defend against the threat – resources that could not be used in offensive systems. That led directly to the low-level penetration requirement, and the B-1 Bomber.

Most of the American aircraft manufacturers were involved to some degree in trying to secure the contract for this new aeroplane. The winning design would be built around the Boeing SRAM (Short Range Attack Missile), a very modern weapon ready for deployment, and the rotary launcher system used in the B-52 bomber. This weapon arrangement, and the fact that the weapons load was 15 per cent of aircraft weight as opposed to only 5 per cent for the B-52, gave the Rockwell International team the contract. It is ironic that the Air Launched Cruise Missile developed by Boeing and another major weapon for the B-1 were the main reasons given for the cancellation of the B-1 project by the Carter administration.

The variable-geometry wing was necessary from the inception because requirements for short take-off, high wing loading and Mach 2 speed. Much of the technical data and design were derived from the F-111 programme. The wing/body blending was selected to increase the internal volume for fuel and to increase the strength of the airframe. The wing carry-through box is a massive structure built of

▼ **A B-1B makes a low-speed pass over the field with gear down and wings extended.**

▼ **A number of feeding tubes resupply a B-1B bomber** on the ground, preparing it for flight.

titanium which carries the wing load on the pivot-pins. The landing gear is also attached to the box. The wings are designed and built to last for 30 years, but if necessary the wing pivot-pins can be removed to install new wings.

The first three B-1s had a crew escape module to contain the four crew members. The module was cut loose from the airframe by explosives and driven away by rockets. After clearing the fuselage, fins were deployed to stabilize the pod, and air bladders cushioned the landing. Further testing revealed that that the module was unstable in some conditions, and it was a very expensive item. By aircraft number four it was replaced with conventional ejection seats. This reduced the cost and the weight of the aircraft.

ENGINES

The engines for the B-1 had to produce adequate power in both the high-altitude supersonic regime, and in high subsonic, low-altitude flight. This mixed requirement needed an efficient fanjet, and General Electric produced variations of the F-101 to meet the challenge.

The General Electric F-101 engine is a high-bypass turbofan of 17,000 lb thrust. With full afterburner, it produces 30,000 lb of thrust. Note that this engine produces twice as much thrust with only 15% of the size and less fuel than the J79 engine in the F-104 *Starfighter*. Also, at low altitude, the engine is nearly smokeless. It is also very efficient in low-altitude flight. Later models of this engine have been chosen to power the USAF F-15 and F-16. The B-1B can maintain flight if only one engine is operating.

The speed requirement was reduced to Mach 1.4, with the emphasis on high subsonic speed with the B-1B. The supersonic speed is available, but it is no longer a design requirement. For this reason, the air inlets were changed to reduce the weight and cost of the engine nacelles. The fixed air-inlet surfaces were also set up to trap or reflect radar waves so that they would not return to the radar search unit. This stealth improvement could be gained only by reducing the speed requirement. But a change in this requirement would cause design changes throughout the aircraft system.

The B-1 is supposed to be able to take off within four minutes of an alert. It also has to function without ground support, except for fuel. Each nacelle houses an APU (Auxiliary Power Unit) for starting the engine. With two APUs, all four engines can be started simultaneously, and either APU can start any engine. All other aircraft system power comes from generators attached to the engines, hydraulic power from engine driven pumps, and bleed air from the main engines.

▼ **The system operators station inside the B-1B bomber has a seemingly bewildering array of instrumentation to monitor and control a very large number of sophisticated attack and defence systems.**

The second prototype B-1A crashed on 29 August, 1984, and Rockwell chief test pilot Doug Benefield was killed in that crash. The cause was attributed to pilot error in that fuel was not transferred between forward and aft tanks to maintain the correct centre of gravity. The wings were swept forward for control testing, causing the plane's centre of gravity to be out of safe bounds. As the airspeed decreased to about 140 knots, the plane pitched up into an out-of-control position. An explosive bolt failed to function, and the crew module landed in a nose down position.

During low-level flight the bomber is subject to a lot of stress from turbulence. Because of the length of the plane, this can be much greater in the cockpit than the actual turbulence would indicate. Force levels up to +4g and −2g can result in only light turbulence. The B1 uses small aerofoils on the fuselage near the front to dampen out vertical whipping of the airframe. These small controls are driven by a "low altitude ride control" system, and can be moved at up to 200 degress per second. Pilots report that with it in operation the B1 is very smooth to fly at low level. The rudder has a small section at the bottom that controls yaw movement. This arrangement was necessary to prevent crew fatigue and increase the life of the airframe.

AVIONICS

The avionics carried by the B1 is not a total package designed into a "system" for installation. The bomber was designed to accept off-the-shelf items, with later conversion to employ "systems" when they became available. The B1 is equipped with four redundant data busses, and electrical multiplexing to carry information around the aircraft. Multiplexing involves carrying several signals on one wire, like carriages of a train. Each segment is coded to get off at the right place. Telephone systems use this method to carry multiple voice signals along one pair of wires. In the B1 it is reported to have saved 130 km (80 miles) of wire and 1,360 kg (3,000 lb) weight.

The B1 carries a staggering array of sensors, aerials and electronic equipment. An entire book could be devoted to just the electronic systems aboard this aircraft. In systems, there is an Offence Avionics System, a Defence Avionics System, Navigation and Position System, redundant Flight Control Systems, Low Altitude Flight System, dual channel, multi-mode Doppler-pulse radar system, and all types of jamming equipment. An entire complement of military and civil communications and navigation radios are carried. There is nothing left to chance in equipping this aircraft to carry out the job of nuclear bombardment if it becomes necessary.

WEAPONS

The internal weapons load is carried on three rotary launchers mounted in three weapons sections. Each launcher holds eight of the AGM-69 Short Range Attack Missiles with one warhead each. Each missile has a range of up to about 170 km (105 miles) and can carry a 200-kilotonne weapon. All 24 weapons can be released in less than a minute. During penetration these missiles can be used to clear the way through defended airspace if necessary.

The forward weapons bay is large enough to carry the Air Launched Cruise Missile, with eight of them on one rotary launcher. This reduces the number of weapons in that bay (to only eight), but the rest of the space is available for an extra fuel tank.

◀ **A front view of the large B-1B bomber in flight.**

▲ **A B-1B flies with its wings swept forwards. The body of the aircraft has three weapons sections and can carry nearly 40,000 kg (90,000 lbs) of weapons and fuel.**

can be housed there, but it is believed that external loads will not be carried on a low-level penetration mission.

Large warhead nuclear weapons can also be dropped from low-level flight. The weapon uses a parachute to reduce its speed to about 95 km/h (60 mph), giving the aircraft time to escape the detonation. Up to 38 of the B-83 nuclear weapons can be carried, with 24 of them in the internal weapons bay and 14 external. In the Soviet Union there are only about 2,000 nuclear targets, so that the expected fleet of 100 B-1s has the ability to target all of them, and have one-third more weapons on stand-by. This is an extremely formidable force. The B-1B can also carry up to 98 of the Mk 84 conventional iron bombs, if it should ever be necessary.

The gross weight of the B-1B production aircraft was increased to carry 38,556 kg (85,000 lb) more fuel and weapons than the B-1A model. The empty weight increased very little for this gain, although the increase did cause a problem with control of the aircraft. It was corrected with the use of a Stability Augmentation System, similar to a Fly-By-Wire system used on other unstable aircraft such as the F-16. The stability system enables full control up to the heaviest weight of the aircraft.

SPECIFICATION

Wingspan:	
MAXIMUM:	4,175.76 cm (137 ft)
MINIMUM:	2,377.44 cm (78 ft)
Wingsweep angle:	15° to 67½°
Length:	4,480.56 cm (147 ft)
Height:	1,036.32 cm (34 ft)
Weight:	
MAXIMUM FOR TAKEOFF:	216,367.2 kg (477,000 lb)
EMPTY WEIGHT:	78.019.2 kg (172,000 lb)
Maximum weapons load:	56,700 kg (125,000 lb)
Engines:	Four F-101 turbofans
Engine Thrust:	Dry, 17,000 lb
WITH AFTERBURNING	30,000 lb
Speed:	
LOW-LEVEL:	Mach 0.85
HIGH-ALTITUDE:	Mach 1.4
Service Ceiling:	49,000 ft
Unrefuelled Range:	6,500 nautical miles

The first operational unit of B-1Bs was stationed at Dyess AFB, outside of Abilene, Texas. The unit began training for the new aircraft in early 1985. It is said about the B-1 that it will have been a success even if it is never flown in the role for which it was planned and built. Let all of us hope it is finally an immense success.

B-2 STEALTH BOMBER

The B-2 bomber is said to be the USA's most famous secret. Everybody knows about the aircraft, but just try to find out something specific – such as how fast it flies. Everything about the aircraft except its existence is secret and is going to stay that way. The shape of the plane is a unique "bat", or flying wing. The shape is designed to maximize stealth, and still provide a large volume for fuel and bombs. The flying wing is a Northrop design dating back to 1929, and is a book in itself.

COMBAT ROLE

The B-2 type is a strategic, long-range, heavy "stealth" bomber. It is meant to be invisible to enemy sensors and radar, and to be able to penetrate the most sophisticated air defences in the world at all altitudes. Stealth is an ability, in the present use of the word, and an aircraft can have more stealth, or less stealth. It is reported that the B-2 bomber has much more stealth than the F-117 *Stealth Fighter* that performed so well over Baghdad during the Gulf War. Yet the stealth ability of the plane has come under criticism since then as not being stealthy enough.

The current advantages of stealth combined with modern precision weapons have revolutionized modern war, at least for the present time. The F-117 bombed downtown Baghdad with impunity in spite of the city being the most heavily defended place in the world at that time. The stealth aircraft simply could not be detected with the means available to the enemy. It also meant that all the planes (stealth) were dropping bombs on their own without

▼ **A B-2 over the desert mountains in the American West on its sixth test flight.**

▶ **A close-up view form the flying boom operator's station during aerial refueling operations over the western United States. Note the angles of the air inlets match the wing sweep.**

needing four times as many other planes along for support.

The B-2 *Stealth Bomber* carries ten times the payload of the F-117, for five times the unrefuelled range. This payload can be in the form of conventional weapons or nuclear bombs. The stealth gives it the ability to survive in a hostile environment to deliver the bombs to the target.

The major materials used in building the B-2 are composites; the types and amounts are secret. It has been reported that the development of composite technology for this aircraft will be of major use for non-military applications in the coming years. New methods and new materials are providing a new generation of composites. Composites have reduced the weight of the B-2 airframe by 25–50 per cent, as compared to conventional metals.

The first B-2 *Stealth Bomber* made its maiden flight on 17 October, 1989. Since that time at least two more have joined the first one in the test-flight programme. Press releases have reported that the B-2 has reached an altitude of 45,000 ft and an airspeed of about 400 knots. Design goal is 50,000 ft altitude and high subsonic airspeed.

ENGINES

The engines used in this bomber are four General Electric F118-GE-100s rated at about 19,000 lb of thrust. They are derived from the ones used in the F-14 and B-1B. They are buried in the fuselage to reduce their visibility to radar and heat sensors. Large amounts of air are used to cool the engines and to mix with the exhaust gas to reduce the heat signature. If afterburners are installed, it has not been reported.

The range of the B-2 is listed as 9,665 km (6,000 miles), or 16,093 km (10,000 miles) with one mid-air refuelling. With air refuelling the range is limited only by the ability of the two-person crew. Provision is made for a third crew member if required by future missions.

The maximum weight is given as 170,554 kg (376,000 lb). This is a big aircraft, and it carries over 18,000 kg (40,000 lb) of weapons. The weapons

▶ B-2 bomber in flight over the American West. Notice that the engine exhaust are on top of the rear fuselage and the left control is deflected to begin to roll to the left.

SPECIFICATION	
Wingspan:	5,242.56 cm (172 ft)
Length:	2,103.12 cm (69 ft)
Height:	518.16 cm (17 ft)
Weight:	Not available
Maximum:	57,600 kg (375,000 lb)
Engines:	Four General Electric G118-GE-100s
Engine Thrust:	19,000 lb each
Maximum Speed:	High subsonic
Range (unrefuelled):	9,655.8 km (6,000 miles)
Service Ceiling:	50,000 ft
Weapons Load:	18,144 kg (40,000 lb)

available include nuclear, conventional precision bombs, stand-off missiles, and maritime weapons. The design allows for a wide variety of weapons to be carried on the aircraft.

The B-2 is designed to require far less maintenance per flight hour than previous aircraft. Because of the high cost of maintenance, all manufacturers of new aircraft have taken this problem seriously. News releases report that this goal is met and exceeded in the test programme.

The heart of the B-2 is the electronics systems carried by the bomber, and very little information is not classified. It is reported that this machine carries the latest class of radar, offensive and defensive electronic warfare systems, and precision navigation equipment. It is not expected that much information will be released any time soon.

The B-2 *Stealth Bomber* is advancing air warfare from massed means to precision means. This aircraft is designed to survive against sophisticated air defence systems, and to deliver a weapon against a selected target. Until a countermeasure is developed, only an aircraft such as the B-2 has the ability to carry out this kind of task really effectively and return to base safely.

▼ **Four for the force: production of USAF/Northrop B-2 stealth bombers continues at Northrop's final assembly plant in Palmdale, California. Funds for continuing production are not always assured.**

F-22 ADVANCED TACTICAL FIGHTER

A consortium of American aircraft manufacturers – Lockheed, General Dynamics and Boeing – teamed up to compete for the first American fighter of the 21st century. In August 1991 this group was selected to develop its YF-22A Advanced Tactical Fighter to replace the F-15 *Eagle* as the air superiority fighter of the future. The F-22 represents a significant design and stealth improvement over the F-117 *Stealth Fighter*, and performance beyond the ability of today's fighters.

The lead time to field a new generation of fighter is lengthy. Fifty-four months were devoted to a demonstration and validation programme. During that time the design, construction and flight testing of two prototype aircraft were completed. Flight tests against the competing YF-23A were also made. This new air superiority aircraft is designed to overcome the new Soviet-made MiG-29 and Su-27, as well as any other fighter in the world today. It must also survive in action where advanced Soviet-supplied missiles are in use. It is expected to be greatly outnumbered also, because the Soviets produced more MiG-29s in the last five years than the US has produced F-15s in the last 15 years.

The F-15 and F-14 designs will be 30 years old by the time this new aircraft is operational in 2005. The Soviet Union put three new fighters into operation since the F-14/15 were conceived. The F-22 is expected to provide air superiority well into the 21st century against these aeroplanes, as well as against the advanced designs the Soviets were known to be developing. To accomplish this task the F-22 will use stealth technology to avoid being seen by sensors, have long-range internal fuel capacity, and exceptional performance. The airspeed capability includes "supercruise", the ability to cruise at supersonic speed without using afterburners, which greatly increases the range of the aircraft. A full package of electronic counter-measures is included to deal with any threat to the aircraft.

The advanced weapons handling system suggests enhanced killing power with the AIM-120A Advanced Medium Range Air-to-Air Missile, as well as present-day missiles. Advanced radar and avionics allow the F-22 to see the enemy first, to launch missiles first, and to destroy the enemy. After the first missile launch the F-22 is expected to perform better than any other fighter in direct air-to-air combat. It will achieve this through the superb manoeuvrability demonstrated by the fighter,

▼ **About to touch down, a breaking parachute is not needed to bring the YF-22 to a stop.**

▲ A YF-22 in flight.

and the greatly improved avionics and weapons control systems. The F-22 is also being designed to "add on" the ground-attack role. The information about this role is not yet available, but because of the large wing area and powerful engines a very heavy bomb load can be expected.

ADVANCED TECHNOLOGY

The design of the F-22 incorporates the latest advances in all related technologies. Fibre optics, digital computers and integrated engine-nozzle controls will be used in the flight-control system. The two-dimensional, thrust-vectoring engine nozzles are controlled by the flight-control system and are transparent to the pilot. Thrust vectoring gives the aircraft about twice the roll rates at low speed as without it. At Mach 1.4 the roll rate is improved by about one-third.

Maximum use will be made of Very High Speed Integrated Circuits in the avionics equipment to reduce the number of parts, weight and cost. Fibre optics are also used for data transmission within the airframe to reduce weight while improving performance. The information available to the pilot could be greater than his ability to comprehend it. To prevent this, only information the pilot requests is presented on CRT readouts.

Some of the goals of the F-22 programme include a reduction in the man hours required to maintain the aircraft. The lower maintenance time compared with the F-15 will reduce the airlift requirement of an F-22 squadron to one-third of that required by an F-15 squadron. The reliability of the F-22 is supposed to be double, and the mission rate increased by one-and-a-half over the F-15.

▼ A view of the YF-22 from the tanker boom operators position.

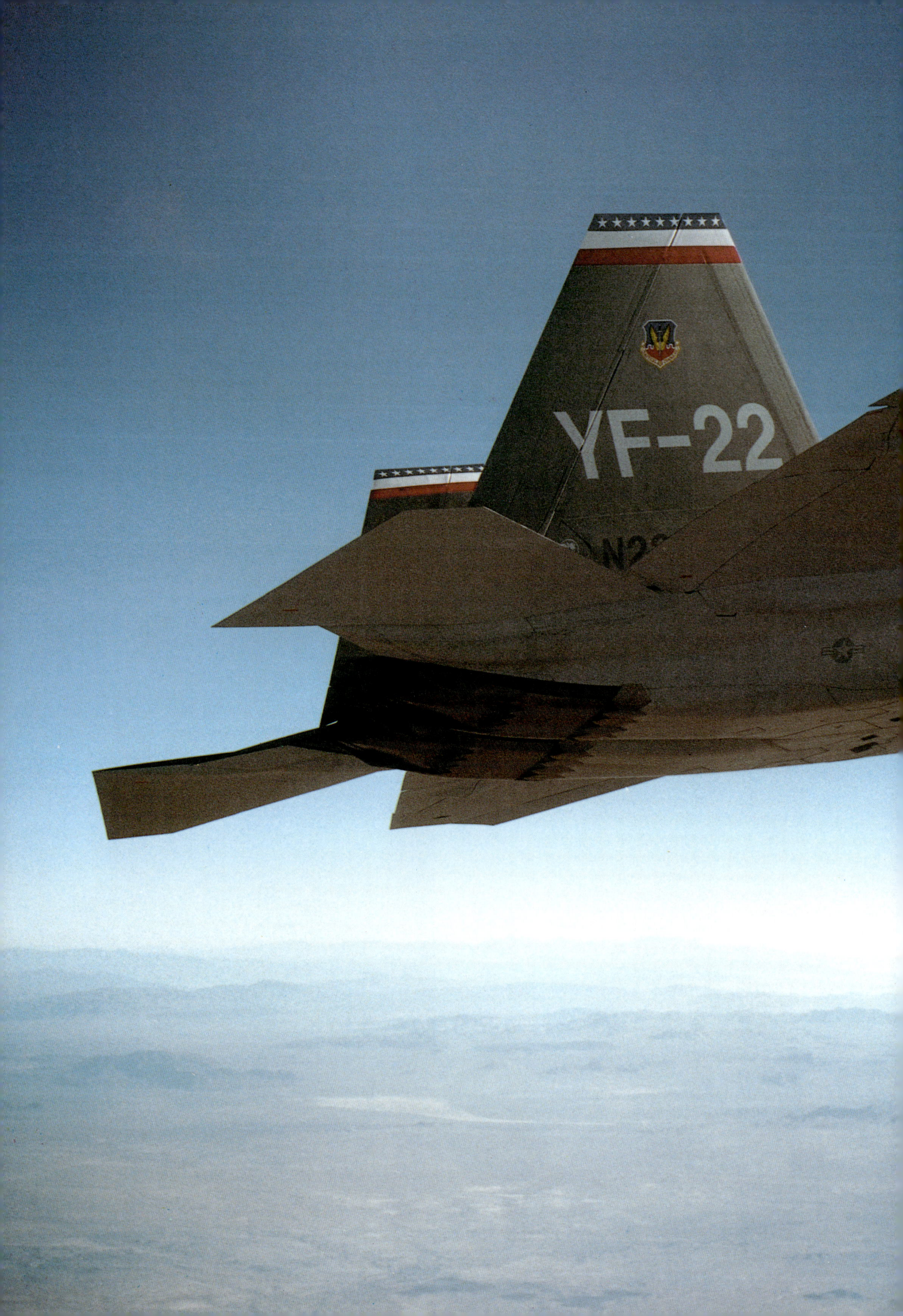
YF-22

SPECIFICATION

WINGSPAN:	1,310.64 cm (43 ft)
LENGTH:	1,955.80 cm (64 ft 2 in)
HEIGHT:	540.77 cm (17 ft 9 in)
EMPTY WEIGHT:	12,700.8 kg (28,000 lb)
MAXIMUM WEIGHT:	Not available
ENGINES:	Pratt & Whitney YF119 or General Electric YF120
ENGINE THRUST:	Approximately 35,000 lb with afterburner
MAXIMUM SPEED:	Mach 1.6+
MAXIMUM RANGE:	Not available, air refuelling capable
COMBAT RADIUS:	Not available, but greater than the F-15
SERVICE CEILING:	Not available, but greater than 50,000 ft

◀ A YF-22 in flight over the American West.

▶ The YF-22 going past vertical onto its back during the flight test procedures.

As compared to the F-15, the F-22 will require only about half the support costs of maintenance, manpower and spare parts. The F-22 will also be self-sufficient, with on-board oxygen and inert gas generators, and an auxiliary power unit (APV) for engine starting and electrical-hydraulic power.

ENGINES

The F-22 development will have two different engines available for tests: the Pratt and Whitney YF119 and the General Electric YF120. Both engines give the F-22 supercruise (supersonic speed without afterburner) ability at about Mach 1.6. The thrust of the new engines is about 10 lb for every pound they weigh. This is an improvement of about 25% over the F-15/16 engines. Which engine the F-22 will utilize has not yet been decided, and both engines are superb. The engine/airframe efficiency allows the F-22 to fly faster than an F-15 while burning only two-thirds of the fuel.

The flight control system is a totally integrated, fly-by-wire system with the pilot inside the loop. The computer moves the controls faster than a pilot ever could, so the pilot is relieved of some of the work of flying. The pilot says where he wants to go and the computer decides how the controls are best positioned to get there. The initial computer program required 50 specialists 30 months to write using the best flight simulators available. Later programs became even larger as flight test data was incorporated to improve the control system.

Lightweight composite structures and plastic materials are used in about one-third of the prototype F-22. The production model will employ more of these materials. Thermoplastic is used to make items such as the landing gear door and other parts which are not subjected to high temperatures. New polyamide resins are used in graphite composites and have two to three times the temperature tolerance of composites used five years earlier. These materials allow very complicated shapes to be fabricated at a lower cost, with less weight, and they do not reflect radar waves.

The US Navy is considering the F-22 as a Strike Fighter for the year 2000. The Navy requires an all-weather attack aircraft with a robust fighter capability. The airframe must be suitable for carrier operations or it will not be considered. The fleet air defence role demands a versatile, capable, fighter, and the F-22 will best meet these requirements during the early years of the 21st century.

▼ **A YF-22 refuels while the F-16 flies escort.**

YF-23 NORTHROP FIGHTER

The Northrop/McDonnell Douglas YF-23A was the second aeroplane competing in the Advanced Tactical Fighter programme. The YF-23 was not selected by the USAF and most likely will not be produced in any numbers.

The Northrop craft is somewhat larger than the competing YF-22, but is much the same in capability. The engines, which are also competing for use, are the same as used in the YF-22. They give the plane the ability to cruise at supersonic speed without using afterburners. The Northrop design incorporates a large amount of composite material, including a one-piece fuselage part that covers both engines. The percentage of composite is not known.

▼ The only two existing YF-23s in formation over the Edwards flight facility.

▲ A side view of YF-23 showing the large one-piece composite engine cover. A major material for this fighter is composites. Note the large leading edge slats that contribute to the planes' maneuverability.

It appears that Northrop was trying to maximize the stealth ability of the YF-23, as seen in the wing and tail angles. The forward fuselage chimes resemble the Lockheed SR-71 fuselage. Weapons were also carried inside the body on a hydraulically operated weapons platform.

The YF-23A is a very sleek and powerful fighter. With the avionics package developd for the ATF it would be a formidable air superiority fighter. Armed with an internal cannon, short range AIM-9 *Sidewinders* and medium range AIM-120 advanced missiles it would supersede the F-15 *Eagle* in its role. Unfortunately, not all aircraft that are designed can be produced, and this one was not selected as the USAF Advanced Tactical Fighter. The YF-23A by Northrop and McDonnell Douglas is a capable aeroplane that may not be built.

▶ Plan (top) view of the YF-23 over the American desert. The tail fins are canted outward enough to read the printing on them. Notice that the engine exhaust is ducted over the top of the aft fuselange to reduce the heat signature.

YF-23 NORTHROP FIGHTER

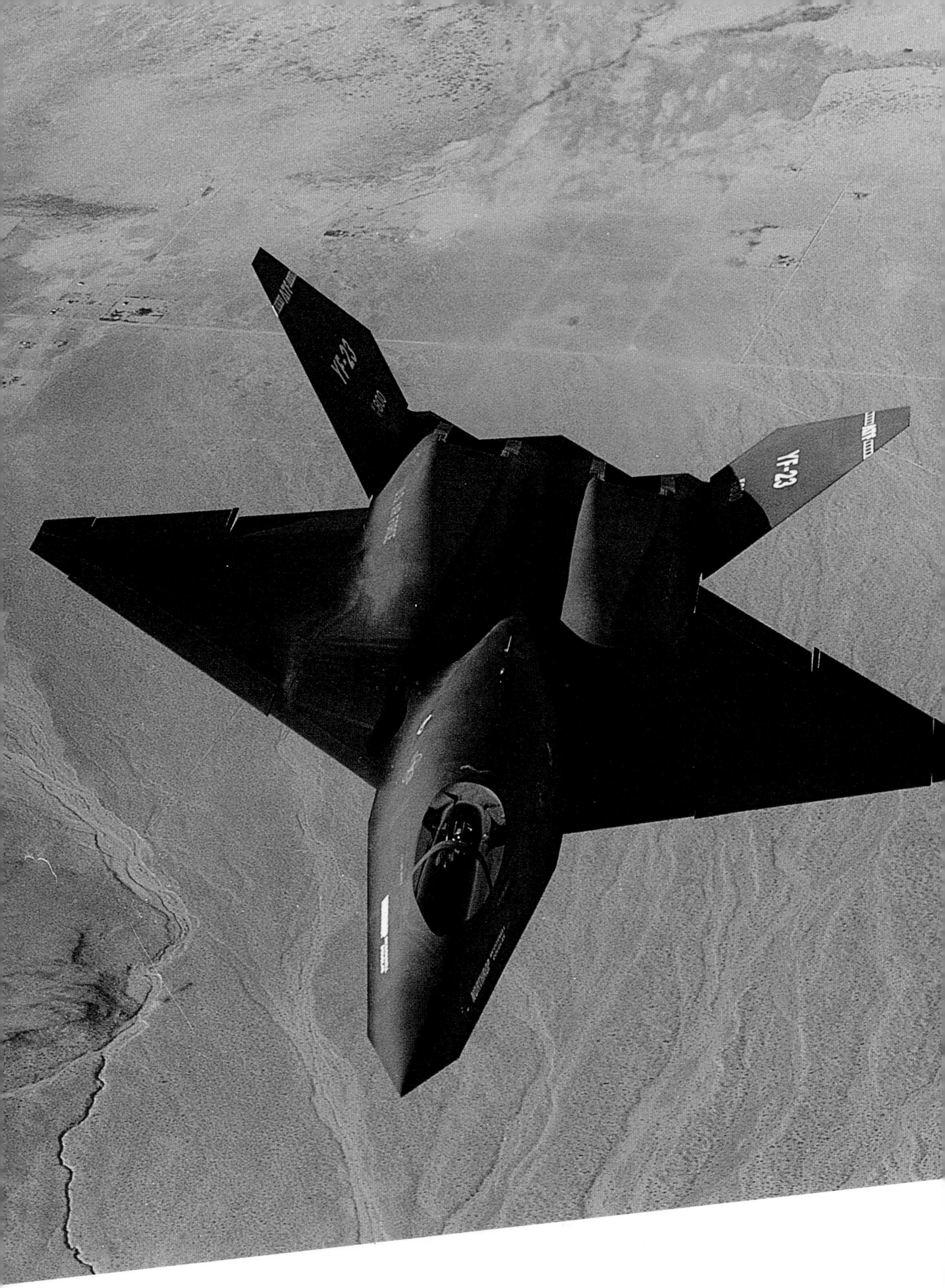
YF-23
YF-23

▲ The two YF-23A prototypes over the Nevada desert. The different paint jobs represent Air Force and Navy colour schemes.

SPECIFICATION	
Wingspan:	1,328.93 cm (43 ft 7 in)
Length:	2,034.13 cm (67 ft 5 in)
Height:	423.67 cm (13 ft 11 in)
Weight:	Not available
Engines:	Two Pratt & Whitney YF-119s or General Electric YF-120s
Engine Thrust:	About 30,000 lb with afterburner
Maximum Speed:	Not available
Cruise Speed:	Mach 1.6 without afterburner
Range:	Unavailable, air refuelling capable
Combat Radius:	Unavailable
Service Ceiling:	Greater than 50,000 ft

F-117 STEALTH FIGHTER

In November 1988 the United States' government announced that a long-rumoured aircraft actually did exist. That announcement ushered the Lockheed F-117A *Stealth Fighter* into the limelight of world attention. This bat-shaped, black fighter is worthy of the limelight because of the technology and capability it brings to aviation.

The contract to design and build a radar-evading stealth fighter was awarded to Lockheed Advanced Development Company in November 1978. This department of Lockheed is the same unit that produced the U-2 spy plane and the SR-71 family of supersonic aircraft. It took only 31 months to produce the plane and achieve its first flight. With a production rate that never went above eight per year, a total of 59 of the planes were delivered to the USAF over the next eight years.

According to Lockheed sources this aircraft is very conventional except for its shape and the security that surrounds the project. Systems were taken from other aircraft in order to not have to develop them for this one. For example, the fly-by-wire (FBW) system is taken from the F-16, and the cockpit from the F/A-18. The shape of the aircraft, and the placement of items (structural items) are arranged to absorb the radar beam, or reflect it in a direction away from the source. A high level of security covers all stealth information, and only general information is available.

The F-117A is powered by two General Electric F-404 turbofan engines. The exhaust is cooled by large amounts of outside air drawn into the engine compartment. The exhaust is also inside the body of the plane, with the exit on top of the trailing edge. The FBW system gives the fighter excellent handling and manoeuvrability. It is reported that actual flying characteristics of the F-117 are very similar to other high-performance fighter aircraft.

WEAPONS

The F-117 has a single weapons bay. A large variety of weapons can be loaded, including laser-guided bombs, tactical munitions dispensers and nuclear weapons. A sophisticated navigation and attack system is integrated into a modern avionics system. The weapons systems are very advanced and have been reported to be able to hit with one bomb what took 9,000 bombs during World War II. The key to success is the stealth ability to avoid detection, and the advanced weapons system.

▼ **F-117 at the holding line ready for takeoff. A second F-117 is in the background.**

▲ F-117 on final approach to a desert test facility. During the Persian Gulf War the fighters were hidden in shelters by this time of day.

The secrecy of the project in developing the stealth fighter has been compared to the project to develop the atomic bomb during World War II. Even the word "stealth" disappeared from the Air Force vocabulary for the duration of the project. The aircraft was never flown during daylight until after the public announcement.

During the development, test flying and creating an operational unit to employ the F-117, the crews lived in Las Vegas. They would fly to Tonopah Air Force Base on Monday, and fly home on Friday. The families of these men were never allowed to know what they were doing, or even where they were. The mission of the F-117 was to be unseen, and unheard, until the bombs it dropped exploded in exactly the right spot and right time.

COMBAT

The aircraft was unveiled to the public on 22 April, 1990. Two of the jets were flown to Nellis Air Force Base in Las Vegas for the occasion. Over 100,000 people came out to view this most talked-about American plane. On 19 August 1990 the entire force was turned out at Langley for a public statement to Saddam Hussein. The message was ignored for five-and-a-half months until the first bombs exploded in downtown Baghdad.

The F-117 *Nighthawk* and the AH-64 *Apache* attack helicopter opened the Gulf air war early in the morning of 17 January, 1990. The F-117 dropped one-ton laser-guided smart bombs, with the first one destroying the AT&T communications building in downtown Baghdad. During this first night the F-117 represented 2.5% of the attacking force and attacked 31% of the targets in Baghdad.

During the Gulf War the F-117s flew more than 1,300 missions. Many of these were over the most heavily defended areas on earth. The F-117 was the only aircraft allowed to attack the downtown area of Baghdad for at least two reasons: the F-117 was invisible to Iraqi radar-controlled guns and missiles, and it possessed the necessary accuracy to bomb exact targets in an area where civilians lived. Only the *Tomahawk* cruise missile joined the F-117 over downtown Baaghdad.

SPECIFICATION	
WINGSPAN:	1,320.79 cm (43 ft 4 in)
LENGTH:	2,00914 cm (65 ft 11 in)
HEIGHT:	378.46 cm (12 ft 5 in)
WEIGHT:	23,814 kg (52,500 lb)
ENGINES:	Two General Electric F404 turbofans
ENGINE THRUST:	16,000+ with afterburner
SPEED:	High subsonic
COMBAT RADIUS:	Unlimited with air refuelling
SERVICE CEILING:	Not available

▼ An F-117 flying high over the winter landscape of the western United States.

◀ F-117 stealth fighter high over the American west.

▼ Close up of the F-117 cockpit area. Notice poor rearward visability and sharp angles of the canopy.

The generals directing the Gulf War did not hesitate to put the most secret American aircraft in the very front of the attacking force. This is in contrast to earlier times when commanders were afraid of losing something so valuable to enemy intelligence. The F-117 is reported to have destroyed 95% of all primary targets in downtown Baghdad. Each attack was recorded on video tape to be replayed later. Each attack was carried out without Combat Air Patrol (CAP) or air defence suppression fighter support. At least one tanker was required for each five F-117 fighters in the attacking force. This plane dramatically changed the way in which high-priority, point targets are attacked from the air.

During the Gulf War the F-117 fighters flew without lights and without radio communications. They were expected to maintain their altitude within a few feet of their asigned altitude, and to drop their bomb within seconds of the assigned time. The extremely close timing was used to avoid anti-aircraft fire and other aircraft in flight. It was also used to make the attack during the time the Iraqi gunners stopped firing to cool the gun barrels.

Praise for the F-117A *Stealth Fighter* has complicated compiling its results. All sources agree that the fighter used far fewer resources to carry out its mission than other fighters. The F-117 flew over 6,900 hours and dropped over 2,000 tonnes of bombs with great precision. During this time in combat, the fleet of 59 fighters did not receive a single scratch from hostile fire. Stealth technology is now a proven weapon of war.

▼ Two F-117 Stealth Fighters return at dawn to their shelter. The F-117 normally flies only at night.

V-22 OSPREY

The art of vertical takeoff and landing has been well established by a technical marvel, the modern helicopter. However, the need for greater speed in level flight has led to different ways of achieving this. One method is to tilt the entire wing, and another is to tilt just the engines and propellers. Bell and Boeing constitute the Tiltrotor team in the United States. After many failed and almost failed attempts by different companies to design and build a practical vertical takeoff and landing airplane, the Bell/Boeing team has the V-22 *Osprey* tiltrotor aircraft.

RADICAL DESIGN

The V-22 is a technological leap in aircraft design. With the ability to takeoff in a vertical mode with engines and rotors pointed upwards, then tilting them to horizontal for turboprop flight, the *Osprey* allows a great strategic mobility. It can self-deploy over 2,100 nautical miles.

It is a quiet and fast, and could be cheaper in the long run because of its unique abilities. The US Marine Corps wants and needs this aircraft.

Since World War II ended, the American aviation industry has produced several vertical takeoff aircraft. The British aerospace industry produced the *Harrier* as the first successful vertical takeoff jet fighter. However, the jet thrust used in the *Harrier* was not acceptable for a troop-lift machine. The tilt prop/rotor was the solution, and two billion dollars were spent by the Government to bring it to reality.

In 1990 the Bell/Boeing team was awarded the prestigious Collier Trophy because of the long-term significance of the technology developed in V-22 *Osprey*. The technology has been praised by many prominent people in the aviation community. Some of the advantages of this technology over pure helicopters include much greater speed and longer range. The V-22 type of aircraft could include city centre-to-centre transport of people and freight.

▼ **Although a V-22 *Osprey* looks in some ways strange and inelegant, it represents a two billion dollar investment to produce one of today's most advanced pieces of aircraft technology.**

▲ **A V-22 Osprey in horizontal flight mode as a turboprop airplane. Airspeed when flying is about 400 km/h (250 mph).**

The larger heliports on downtown, buildings would accommodate the V-22 with ease, because the rotors can overhang the edge of the building. This is equally true on the flight deck of a carrier.

The V-22 is a fully instrument flight-capable aircraft and has both primary and automatic flight-control systems. The automatic mode has been used to make carrier landings, and might be able to bring the machine to a roof-top heliport even when the building is enclosed in clouds. The reliability of the system is being proved at the present time through a six-aircraft, $1.8 billion development contract with the US Naval Air Systems Command.

Two of the V-22 *Ospreys* were used to confirm shipboard compatibility during tests in January 1991. The two *Ospreys* flew about 90 km (60 miles) offshore to conduct operations aboard the USS *Wasp* (LHD-1), a US Navy amphibious assault ship. Operations proved that the V-22 would safely and efficiently operate aboard the assault ships. One necessary concession was a small exhaust deflector to reduce hot gasses hitting the deck. Future *Ospreys* will have an articulated deflector that will also provide some jet thrust in level flight. For storage aboard ship, the rotors of both engines fold and the wing then turns 90 degrees to align with the fuselage.

The *Osprey* is said to be very easy to fly. Takeoff is similar to a helicopter without rotor torque, because of the counter-rotating rotors. Translation to horizontal mode requires several seconds, during which the aircraft accelerates to winged-flight speed.

▶ **An Osprey about to touch down during shipboard qualification trials.**

Deceleration to a hover is just the opposite, reducing the airspeed to near zero as the rotors are tilted. The V-22 will hover around just like a helicopter and is stable in the hover mode. Top speed of the *Osprey* is not available. However, it has been flown up to 400 km/h (250 mph) at 8,300 ft altitude. This speed is just one milestone of the test programme, and speed should ultimately approach 480 km/h (300 mph).

The gross weight of the *Osprey* depends upon the mission, and manner of takeoff. In the helicopter mode the weight is limited to 21,546 kg (47,500 lb). If a runway is available the props can be tilted forward about 20 degrees and a rolling takeoff performed. In this takeoff the gross weight can be increased to 8,450 kg (55,000 lb). Runway requirement is about 150 m (500 ft) and the additional lift is generated by the wings.

HI-TECH PLANES

The maximum gross weight for the V-22 *Osprey* is 27,442.8 kg (60,500 lb) on a self-deployment mission. Auxiliary fuel tanks are loaded inside the cabin and no passengers or cargo are carried. The range of this mission is about 2,100 nautical miles.

SPECIFICATION	
ROTOR DIAMETER:	1,158.24 cm (38 ft), each rotor
MAXIMUM DIAMETER:	2,578 cm (84.58 ft)
LENGTH:	1,747.42 cm (57.33 ft)
FUSELAGE WIDTH:	180.44 cm (5.92 ft) internal
ENGINES:	Two Allison T406 turboshafts
SHAFT HORSEPOWER:	6,150 shp
MAXIMUM SPEED:	
HELICOPTER MODE:	160 km/h (100 mph)
AEROPLANE MODE:	442 km/h (275 mph)
RANGE, INTERNAL FUEL:	1,000 nautical miles
CEILING:	Not available
AIR REFUELLING:	Not available, testing started

The cargo capacity and range are determined by mission. With a full load of 24 combat-armed troops, the range of the craft is about 500 nautical miles. With full internal fuel the range is about 1,000 nautical miles, and the number of troops is reduced. The internal cargo capacity is about 9,000 kg (20,000 lb). Either cargo hook can carry 4,500 kg (10,000 lb), or both hooks in tandem can carry 6,800 kg (15,000 lb). Using both hooks in tandem also allows external loads to be carried at speeds of up to 200 knots.

The cabin of the *Osprey* is free from obstructions and will seat 24 combat-equipped troops. The tail is a full-width hydraulically operated loading ramp which is lowered to provide passenger and cargo loading. Anything that will fit inside the cabin can be loaded through the ramp door.

ROTORS

The rotors are three-bladed fibreglass and graphite construction, a type of material that is being widely

▼ **A V-22 Osprey is inspected as it waits on the airstrip during trials.**

▲ **The V-22 proprotors folded. The entire wing then pivots until parallel with the fuselage. Folding into a compact package is necessary for storage aboard carriers.**

used for advanced rotor blades in the helicopter industry. The fibreglass blades have a longer life and are less subject to failure from damage. Even if shattered they retain most of their mass and may allow an emergency landing. Cracks do not spread in fibreglass as they do in metal.

With two rotors separated by over 12 m (40 ft), a failure in one engine would be a catastrophe. The engines are coupled by a segmented steel shaft that is unloaded and turning at full RPM during normal operations. If one engine loses power the shaft is automatically engaged to maintain balanced lift between the two rotors. The engines are Allison T406-AD-400 turboshafts capable of producing 6,150 shp (shaft horse-power) at sea level. The engines are down-rated to 4,200 or 5,290 shp for single-engine operations. The pilot reaches the aircraft power limit before reaching the engine's maximum power output. This has been called "pilot down rating," and is normal in modern high-powered helicopters.

For shipboard operations it is necessary to stow the rotors, and rotate the wing to align with the fuselage. These operations are automated and require 90 seconds to complete. The rotors are first folded back along the engine nacelle, then the nacelles are rotated to the horizontal position. The wing is unlocked and rotates on a carousel until parallel with the fuselage. When the *Osprey* is folded up it can be moved by elevator to the inside of the carrier ship.

The *Osprey* is the first military aircraft to have full colour video screens for all pilot information. The cockpit does not have gauges, meters, radio panels or such items. All the functions are displayed on the four multi-function television-type screens. All flight and navigation information is also displayed on the same screens. Instead of toggle switches, lighted push-button switches are used. Mounted in the lower-centre of the console are two digital data processor control display units (CDU). Both pilots can assess all aircraft subsystems from this unit, as well as carry out all functions from starting engines to navigation.

The V-22 *Osprey* is being developed by the team of Bell Helicopter Textron, Inc., and Boeing Helicopters of Philadelphia, Pennsylvania. The entire tiltrotor concept is developing at a brisk rate and we expect to see more of the *Osprey* in the future.

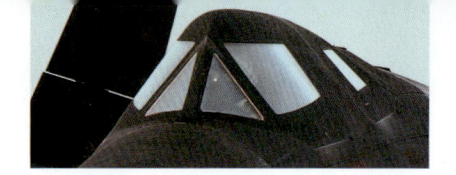

SR-71 BLACKBIRD

For many people the SR-71 represents the epitome of aircraft in the world today. The SR-71, and the family in the same mould, is unequalled in ability – and secrecy – in aviation. Books are devoted to this plane, and yet the top speed attained by the SR-71 is still secret. It has now been removed from military service and has become a museum piece, but its reconnaissance package is also still secret. It is not expected to become unclassified for many years.

The aircraft in this family were conceived in the late 1950s by Kelly Johnson, Director of the Lockheed Advanced Development Company, after development of a liquid hydrogen powered plane was cancelled. This aircraft, the "A" series, was one of several competing designs funded by the USAF and the CIA for a high-performance aircraft. The A-12 (12th in the series) design resulted in the first plane in the world to cruise at Mach 3+.

CONSTRUCTION

The plane is built from BEta B-120, a titanium alloy developed by Lockheed and the Titanium Metals Corporation. The B-120 alloy weighs about half as much as stainless steel, yet is just about as

▼ **An SR-71 Blackbird in the landing pattern at a test facility.**

strong. The problems of working with titanium are immense, but it is the best metal for the structure. At the time that the planes were being produced, composites were not available, so only a small percentage of the aircraft is made of plastic. It is reported that 93% of the empty weight of the aircraft is titanium, but this has not been released. It is about 17,200 kg (38,000 lb) for the A-12, and 27,200 kg (60,000 lb) for the SR-71.

Titanium is totally incompatible with certain elements, including chlorine, fluorine and cadmium. When titanium that has been exposed to such elements gets hot (315°C/600°F) it becomes brittle. This problem caused failure of some parts and was finally traced to the water supply, which had a high chlorine content in the summer, and to cadmium-plated tools used by the mechanics. Distilled water was then used to wash parts and cadmium-plated tools were removed from the tool boxes.

Normally, the wing panels on the plane would have distorted out of shape due to high heat at Mach 3+. To prevent this the panels are corrugated to allow expansion without warping. As the metal heats, the corrugations deepen by a few thousandths of an inch without other movement. The wings are also fuel tanks, and special sealants were developed to allow expansion and still keep the fuel inside the tanks. The fuel cools the wings, but causes warping of the wings when the fuel level is low. There is no reported solution for this problem, but it is said to be acceptable.

The larger empty weight of the SR-71 reflects a somewhat larger aircraft for the Strike/Reconnaissance role, and the increased fuel capacity. Over 45,500 litres (12,000 US gallons) of the special JP-7 fuel are carried in the SR-71. It was developed by the Shell Oil Company and is used as a heat sink for the entire aircraft, and as hydraulic oil. Special hydrocarbons were added to the fuel to give it some lubrication qualities in pumps and valves. The fuel is so stable that a special igniter is injected with it to start the main engines and the afterburner.

ENGINES

The first A-12 was transported on lorries to the Groom Lake flight test facility in Nevada for re-assembly and preparation for flight. Lockheed test pilot Lou Schalk made the first official flight on 26 April, 1961. The engines powering this plane were Pratt & Whitney J-75s instead of the J-58s, which were still under development. The J-75s allowed a maximum speed of only Mach 1.2, but this was enough speed for flight testing to take place.

Seven months later the first J-58 engines were available and used. The J-58 has been described in some publications as a "turboramjet" engine. It may well be considered as such by some people, but it is not officially described that way by Pratt & Whitney Corporation. The conditions in which this engine must operate were unique and were more demanding than for the MiG-25. Lockheed's Kelly Johnson says that this was the time when flight test problems really began.

▼ **The returning Blackbird.** Tires are subject to extreme heat and wear. They will be replaced before the next mission. It requires hours for the airplane to cool down after a high-speed mission.

The J-58 engine design was started years earlier for a Navy project that was cancelled. It was just in time for the Lockheed A-12 project. All three variations of the family use this engine. The J-58 is unique in present military use because it is a very high bypass engine. As in the engine used in the Soviet MiG-25, most of the power comes from the afterburner section and not from the engine itself. At maximum power at sea level, the engine develops over 32,000 lb of thrust. It is capable of sustained operation at speeds of Mach 3.2+. At that speed the main engine is providing only about 17.6% of the total thrust, with the remainder coming from the afterburner section. Thrust and drag are critically dependent on the air inlet and spike.

It has been reported that the hardest problem to solve was control of the spike in the air inlet to control the air and shock wave. In certain conditions the spike has to withstand up to 32,000 pounds of force from the air. As the speed changes the spike must be moved fore and aft up to a metre (3 ft) to control the air flow. Over 25,000 hours of wind-tunnel testing were devoted to the nacelle and air inlet. In a test jig a J-79 engine exhaust was used to simulate the temperature and velocity of air entering the engine. Pictures of this test jig with both engines running show the entire aft section of the J-58 engine glowing cherry red.

In flight, the problem was an "unstart" of the nacelle air inlet. This was a loss of control of the air and shock wave resulting in a sudden power loss. The engine did not stop, but began to overheat with the loss of airflow. Ways were soon found to solve the problem and eliminate unstart. One of the solutions was to increase the size of the air bypass doors and to add air suck-in doors. The new doors allowed air to be used to cool the engine and go directly to the exhaust ejector. The nacelle had to be sealed to enabled a 40:1 ram-air pressurization to be delivered to the afterburner section.

The wing of the SR-71 is a delta planform, cantilever design of 2.5% thickness-to-cord ratio. It is a multi-spar type with about two-thirds being used for fuel storage. The leading edge has about 52.6 degrees of sweep, with the trailing edge sweeping forward about 10 degrees. The engines are mounted mid-way out on each wing in spar carry-through hoops. All-moving rudders are mounted on top of each engine nacelle. The rudders are canted in 15 degrees to take advantage of the vortex generated by the fuselage chines.

All of the A-12s and SR-71s are painted black with a special paint. The composition of the paint and related information are still classified. It does, however, contain iron pigment to dissipate electromagnetic energy. The plane has always been called the *Blackbird*.

Heat build-up is a major villain facing the SR-71, and everything inside it. The fuel temperature can be as low as $-68°C$ ($-90°F$) or as high as $315°C$ ($600°F$). To seal fuel lines and connectors, special steel washers had to be invented because "O" rings would not work. All of the tyres were designed by B. F. Goodrich and contain powdered aluminium to dissipate heat. The wheel wells are surrounded by fuel to cool the wheels. The electrical wire used in the plane has to withstand the high temperatures, and special wire had to be devised. Nitrogen gas is used to inflate the tyres and pressurize the fuel tanks. The huge parachute carried in the top aft point of the fuselage seems to be well protected from the heat. As stated before, the fuel is used to cool almost everything in the plane, and as hydraulic fluid for the landing gear and all control surfaces before it is fed to the engine at the rate of 3,630 kg (8,000 lb) per hour.

▼ **An SR-71 in high speed, high altitude flight, with afterburners lit. The pulses are caused by shock waves from the afterburner section.**

SPECIFICATION

CREW:	**Two: pilot and systems operator**
WINGSPAN:	**1,694.18 cm (55 ft 7 in)**
LENGTH:	**3,279.14 cm (107 ft 7 in)**
HEIGHT:	**563.88 cm (18 ft 6 in)**
WEIGHT:	
EMPTY:	**27,216 kg (60,000 lb)**
MAXIMUM:	**63,504 kg (140,000 lb)**
ENGINES:	**Two Pratt & Whitney J-58 turbojets**
THRUST:	**32,000 lb with afterburner**
MAXIMUM SPEED:	**Classified Mach 3.2+**
MAXIMUM RANGE (UNREFUELLED):	**5,632.5km**
	(3,500 miles)
SERVICE CEILING:	**Classified, above 85,000 ft**

The altitude versus airspeed information concerning the SR-71 is still classified information. Maximum speed can be achieved only at very high altitude, and it may be that 80,000 ft represents the lowest altitude for maximum velocity. At sea level a speed of 3,200 km/h (2,000 mph), well below the A-12's top speed, will heat stainless steel to the melting point where it flows with the air stream. Another contradiction with this plane is that under certain conditions increasing speed uses less fuel.

YF-12A

The second version of this plane, the YF-12A, was designed as a fighter/interceptor. It did not carry a gun and all missiles were housed in a weapons bay. The concept was to base the craft inside the USA and still be able to intercept enemy bombers outside the border using the very high speed. Only a few of the YF-12As were constructed before the SR-71 design. The top speed of the A-12 is reported to be Mach 3.6 above 90,000 ft. The speed of the YF-12A was only a little lower, while the SR-71 was only about Mach 3.2+ at 80,000 ft.

Information about numbers and configurations varies from source to source, but it is believed that the first three aircraft were research units. After 15 were delivered that had a strike capability with a one-megaton nuclear bomb carried on the centreline. In 1964 the definitive SR-71 became operational. Most aircraft were the SR-71 version, and the number produced is known to exceed 29. The SR-71 is about 3 m (6 ft) longer than the YF-12A and 14,500 kg (32,00 lb) heavier at maximum weight. The range of the SR-71 without refuelling is given as 5,630 km (3,500 miles). Missions of over 22,500 km (14,000 miles) have been flown to demonstrate the world-wide capability of the airplane – London to New York in one hour and 55 minutes by SR-71.

◀ **A high altitude view of the SR-71. US Air Force markings are seldom displayed on the Blackbirds.**

AH-1 COBRA

The helicopter came of age during the 1950–53 conflict in Korea, and reached maturity in Vietnam. During the Vietnam War a new, capable helicopter gunship for the Army became essential to replace the converted troop ships that were used as gun platforms. Bell Helicopter already had a proposal ready for consideration: the *Cobra* attack helicopter.

During the Vietnam War, beginning in 1967, the Bell *Cobra* AH-1G flew in many roles to support the ground forces. It was used for area suppressive fire during helicopter troop landings, and to provide close fire support for the troops on the ground. It was used for reconnaissance, and to attack anything that moved in free-fire areas. AH-1Gs would fly close fire support for medical-evacuation helicopters, and fire support for search and rescue missions. Late in the war, the *Cobra* flew missions against North Vietnam armour. Anywhere and any time close fire support was needed, the AG-1G was there.

The AH-1G is a single-engined, two-man helicopter designed specifically for the ground-attack role. A two-bladed main and tail rotor give the aircraft agility, speed and a respectable weapons load. The 91-cm (36-in) wide fuselage and the unique rotor head design allows an airspeed up to 190 knots. The *Cobra* has been flown in looping and barrel roll manoeuvres, even though this is outside the flight envelope for normal flight.

WEAPONS

External weapons for the AH-1G are carried on four pylons on the wings, with standard lug attachments. Up to 76 7-cm (2.75-in) rockets can be carried, depending on other loads and the weather. Weapons pods with different weapons also can be carried. These include a 7.62 mm minigun with 1,500 rounds, .50-in calibre machine-guns, and 20 mm cannons of various types. Another weapon is a three barrel 20 mm cannon mounted on the left inside pylon, with 1,000 rounds of ammunition carried in outside packs

▼ **US Army AH-1F.** The exhaust extension mixes cool air with the exhaust gas. The co-pilot/gunner's door is on the left side of the capopy.

▲ A US Marine Corps AH-1W, or "Whiskey" model flying low over very wet land. This model was employed by the Marines in the Gulf War and is the latest model available.

mounted on the fuselage.

The chin turret can be equipped with two weapons; each side can have either a 7.62 mm minigun or a 40 mm grenade launcher mounted in it. Four thousand rounds of 7.62 mm ammunition or 250 40 mm grenades can be carried on each side. The chin turret is normally controlled and fired by the front seat co-pilot/gunner. The pilot can fire the turret weapons only from a fixed forward-firing position. Later model *Cobras* incorporate a helmet-mounted sighting system with which both pilots can aim and fire the turret guns.

The later model AH-1S is a redesigned *Cobra*, better equipped to fly-and-fight in the NOE (Nap Of the Earth) anti-tank environment. The S model uses the uprated Lycoming T-53-L-703 engine of 1,800 shaft horsepower (shp); an increase of 400 shp over the G model.

The S model has a nearly flat plate canopy for reduced sun flash, and is armed with TOW (Tube-launched Optical-tracked Wire-guided) anti-tank missiles. The turret can be mounted with either the 20 mm cannon, or the 7.62/40 mm combination, depending on the production time of the airframe.

The S model is the first *Cobra* to have a Fire Control Computer installed. This system incorporates an Air Data Sensor and greatly increases the accuracy of the weapons. Sensors advise the crew of threat radar and infra-red (IR) sources, such as an incoming missile. A dispenser is mounted opposite the tail rotor to fire flares designed to deflect the missile away from the aircraft.

The TOW mount is available in two- or four-missile units. A normal load for an anti-tank mission would be a total of eight missiles on the two inside pylons. The TOW missile is accurate out to 3,750 metres ($2\frac{1}{3}$ miles), and will penetrate over 500 mm (20 in) of armour. The TOW is guided to target impact by the co-pilot/gunner through his Telescopic Sighting Unit, a stabilized, magnified-view target sight. The gunner has only to maintain the crosshairs on the target, not actually guide the missile. The TOW missile has proved to be an effective weapon against hard, point targets during combat in the Middle East and other conflicts.

The new *Cobras* are equipped with a laser tracker for better target hand-off operations. This system displays the point of laser splash on a heads-up display for the pilot. Along with a Doppler Radar Navigation system, it allows the helicopter to manoeuvre out of sight of the target and have the target in the sight as the helicopter pops up to shoot. The laser range-finder and fire control computer greatly increases the overall accuracy of the rockets and the 20 mm cannon.

Survivability is enhanced with the use of ballistically-tolerant composite main rotor blades (which can tolerate a certain amount of damage) and low IR reflective paint. The hot gasses from the engine are cooled and diffused with air drawn into the exhaust from outside. Normally hot metal is also cooled with this large volume of cool air. An active IR jammer, AN/ALQ-144, is used to confuse IR-seeking missiles. The IR signature of the AH-1S is only about 10% of the unsuppressed signature.

SUPER COBRA

The latest model of the *Cobra* is the AH-1W *Super Cobra*, the "Whiskey" model.
It is a greatly improved version of the AH-1T used by the Fleet Marine Forces. This model is powered by two powerful General Electric T700-GE-401 engines rated at 1,625 shp for a total of 3,250 shaft horsepower. This is probably the most excess power of any helicopter in the world. The Whiskey model will hover out of ground-effect with a maximum load of eight TOW or eight *Hellfire* rockets, and a full load of cannon ammunition with power to spare. The Whiskey model can, on a standard day, takeoff with a full load of weapons on a single engine and climb at 800 ft per minute.

The Whiskey model carries updated electronics and weapons control systems. Both TOW and *Hellfire* missiles can be carried at the same time (other attack helicopters do not have this capability). The three-barrel 20 mm turret cannon can be aimed and fired by either crew member through helmet-mounted sights. Seven hundred and fifty rounds by 20 mm shells are carried. The high-velocity Navy *Phalanx* shell, using a depleted uranium/tungsten steel penetrator in a discarding sabot, can also be

▼ **An AH-1 *Cobra* flies homewards from a daytime training mission.**

used in this gun. This shell gives three times the armour penetration of a standard round.

The AH-1W can carry missiles for air-to-air engagements. The long-range *Sidewinder* and the light *Stinger* can be used in air defence of helicopter troop ships. This is the first time US helicopters have been armed, and allowed to be used, as air-to-air fighters. Future writers will chronicle how this combat turns out. Fighters in recent conflicts have destroyed many helicopters with immunity, but that will probably change with helicopter air-to-air combat qualification.

The Bell AH-1W was employed by the US Marine forces in the Gulf War and successfully engaged Iraqi tanks, including the heavy T-72. The Iraqi forces were soundly defeated wherever the few Marine AH-1W models went into combat. The Whiskey also has an improved infra-red vision system and laser-ranging unit. With Doppler navigation, these systems give the Whiskey a day and night combat capability.

Future improvements planned for the AH-1W include a new four-bladed bearing-less rotor that will increase the weapons payload to 17,690 kg (3,900 lb). A new six-pylon wing will carry the munitions. The new rotor is described as giving ". . . Jet-like smoothness". Clearly, the helicopter gunship has come a long way since 1967 and the AH-1G as used in Vietnam.

▲ **Marine AH-1W over open water. The "W" model is a major improvement over previous Marine version, with much larger power plants, and updated avionics equipment.**

▼ **Three AH-1Fs, sans front seat gunner, in formation over the Texas plant. The "F" model is a greatly improved single engine version of the TOW equipped Cobra.**

▲ **An AH-1F in flight.**
The Cobra carries up to eight TOW anti-tank wire guided missiles.

SPECIFICATION	
CREW:	Two; pilot in rear, co-pilot/gunner in front
ENGINES:	Two General Electric T700-401s
POWER:	1,625 shp
MAXIMUM WEIGHT:	6,690.6 kg (14,750 lb)
EMPTY WEIGHT:	4,626.7 kg (10,200 lb)
LENGTH:	1,306.84 cm (15 ft 2½ in)
HEIGHT:	463.30 cm (15 ft 2½ in)
ROTOR DIAMETER:	1,463.04 cm (48 ft)
SPEED:	170 knots
RANGE:	317 nautical units

◀ **An AH-1 *Cobra*** painted with a heavy camouflage pattern flies on patrol during the Gulf War.

AH-64 APACHE

The Bell AH-1G was the only true helicopter gunship available during the Vietnam War. When the rigid-rotor Cheyenne Advanced Aerial Fire Support system (AAFSS) was cancelled in 1969, a new programme was initiated to study the requirements for an attack helicopter.

The new study led to low-level operations being accepted as the normal and sanctioned method of engaging enemy targets. The huge number of tanks opposing the NATO forces in Western Europe required that this new attack helicopter be primarily an anti-tank weapon system. It would supplement the Bell *Cobra* in that role, and replace the *Cobra* eventually. The *Apache* was born in 1972 in the Hughes Helicopter Company (now McDonnell Douglas) as one answer to the Army requirement. A "fly-off" competition between the Hughes YAH-64 and an advanced *Super Cobra* YAH-63 was decided in favour of the Hughes' machine.

▼ **The nose of an AH-64 displays sensors for the array of electronic vision and targetting devices that the aircraft carries.**

The *Apache* could be considered a third generation attack helicopter, with converted troop ships the first, and the Bell *Cobra* the second. The *Apache* possess all-weather, day-and-night combat operations ability, and high reliability. The fire power carried by the *Apache* can help to defeat very large forces of armoured vehicles.

DESIGN

The *Apache* is a twin-engined helicopter with a four-bladed main and tail rotors. A two-person crew operates the machine, with the pilot in the rear cockpit and a co-pilot/gunner in the forward position. The two positions are separated by a clear anti-blast shield. Flight control is via conventional helicopter controls, with stability augmentation.

The *Apache* is also designed for survivability in combat or accident. The crew cannot eject, and so the aircraft must protect them as much as is practical in the event of accident or being shot down. Also, helicopters are

◀ AH-64 Apache, flown by McDonnell Douglas experimental test pilots, completes an aerobic maneuver.

An auxiliary power unit (APU) provides power for all aircraft systems for ground operation, and air to start the main engines.

WEAPONS

The only gun normally installed in the *Apache* is the 30-mm Chain Gun under the forward chin. It is driven by a bicycle-type chain and fires through a rotating bolt mechanism. It has proved to be an efficient weapon with only the low velocity of the shell being a drawback. There are 1,200 rounds of linkless ammunition carried aboard, and the gun fires at a rate of 625 rounds per minute.

The weapon is controlled primarily through the co-pilot/gunner's Target Acquisition Designation Sight (TADS) system and the Fire Control Computer (FCC). It can also be aimed and fired by either crew member through the helmet-mounted sight. In that mode the gun points to whatever the pilot is looking at. The ability to turn 110 degrees left and right, and to depress 60 degrees gives the gun a wide field of fire. It is a devastating weapon for use against armoured cars and other soft or area targets.

The 2.75-in (70-mm) Folding Fin Aerial Rocket (FFAR) is used for an unguided area fire weapon. The fire control and aiming systems give the rocket much better accuracy at low level than previous ones. Various warheads are available for this rocket, including high explosive, high explosive anti-tank, smoke and sub-munitions dispersing.

The main anti-tank weapon on the AH-64 is the *Hellfire* laser-guided missile produced by the Rockwell International company. Up to 16 of these mis-

expensive and the second goal
is to keep damage to the airframe as low as possible. To achieve this goal every part, system or subsystem was designed to keep the aircraft flying in spite of damage. Some systems are duplicated, others separated as far as practical, or designed to tolerate certain weapon hits. The rotor blades and structure of the body were designed to withstand multiple hits from the 23-mm Soviet cannon. Some critical areas are also protected with the use of armour plate, and the crews' seats are armoured.

The *Apache* is powered by two General Electric T700-GE-701 engines of 1,694 shaft horsepower each. Ample reserve power is available for the helicopter to fly home on one engine. The lack of power that plagued helicopters for many years does not apply to the AH-64 (or other modern helicopters).

▶ 30mm M230 automatic cannon on the McDonnell Douglas AH-64 attack helicopter. The cannon is commonly referred to as "chain gun."

▲ **Two US Army aviators fly a fully armed AH-64 Apache anti-armor helicopter over water while on a training mission from Fort Hood, Texas. The Apache was a star performer in the Persian Gulf War.**

siles can be carried in a heavy attack mission. In the usual mission only 8 *Hellfires* are carried, and the outer-wing pylons are loaded with 19-shot 2.75-in rocket pods. The *Hellfire* missile, equipped with a laser-seeker head, can be programmed to seek a target designed by the gunner, or by any other laser designator. This gives the *Apache* a great deal of flexibility in the engagement of targets.

The *Hellfire* is produced by Rockwell International, and is a 45.4-kg (100-lb), 18-cm (7-in) diameter missile. The seeker can be set to respond to different laser codes to seek one laser splash out of many that may be on the battlefield. The target can be designated by any other laser in an aircraft or on the ground, and several *Hellfires* can be in the air at the same time.

Advanced sensor and weapons control systems include a Pilot's Night Vision Sensor, and a Target Acquisition and Designation Sight. The night vision and infra-red sensing equipment give the pilot the ability to fly at night and in bad weather. The targeting system is the principal aid for the front-seat

▲ **Using advanced detection and targeting systems, the AH-64 Apache helicopter is effective in performing tank-killing missions night and day.**

gunner and includes direct telescopic sighting, infra-red sighting, laser designator, range-finder and tracking. The system can even see through much of the smoke of the battlefield. The helicopter can take full advantage of night and bad weather to operate, and in the Gulf War the night capability was fully exploited.

While the AH-64 *Apache* was not designed with stealth ability, the aircraft was made to reduce certain signatures. The canopy is made up of flat plate sections to reduce sun glint. In the low-level role, a curved canopy would cause a sun flash over a wide area and alert the enemy of its presence. The infrared signature of the engines is greatly reduced by the use of three heat diffusers in the exhaust of each engine. Electronic jammers help to hide the AH-64 from enemy radars.

COMBAT

During the Gulf War the AH-64 and the F-117A *Stealth Fighter* opened the air campaign. Eight AH-64s flew deep into Iraq and, within seconds of a predetermined time, blasted two air-defence radar bases. The two bases had to be knocked out at the same time to prevent other bases from closing the gap created in the radar coverage. All eight *Apaches* returned home without a scratch.

In all of the desert combat only one AH-64 was lost to enemy fire. An *Apache* of Company C, 1-227th Aviation Regiment, 1st Cavalry Division, was shot down on the morning of 25 February in southern Iraq. It is believed to have been hit by a ground-launched missile. In tribute to the qualities of the design, both pilots were able to walk away from the crash, and were rescued, flying strapped to the wing of another *Apache*.

◄ **From a high hover an Apache launches several pairs of 70mm Hydra rockets.**

▲ In a daytime training mission an AH-64 fires the powerful AGM-114 Hellfire anti-tank missile.

The number of tanks and other targets destroyed by *Apaches* during the Gulf War has not yet been released. However, the last major engagement was when retreating Iraqi Republican Guards attacked elements of the 24th Division. An *Apache* battalion, the 1-24th, engaged the enemy force and fired at least 107 *Hellfire* missiles. Thirty-two tanks were reported destroyed, along with over 100 other vehicles. The *Apache* helicopter gunship proved its mettle in that war.

▼ An AH-64 Apache ready for combat in Operation Desert Storm.

SPECIFICATION

Main Rotor Diameter:	1,463.04 cm (48 ft)
Tail Rotor Diameter:	279.50 cm (9 ft 2 in)
Overall Length, rotors turning:	1,772.93 cm (58 ft 2 in)
Maximum Height to top of air data sensor:	464 cm (15 ft 3 in)
Fuselage Width across engine nacelles:	275.84 cm (9 ft ½ in)
Wingspan:	522.73 cm (17 ft 1¾ in)
Engines:	Two General Electric T700-GE-701 turboshafts of 1694 shp each
Weapons Load:	4,536 kg (6,500 lb)
Range:	1,6095 km (1,000 miles), ferry mission
Weight empty:	4,880.7 kg (10,760 lb)
Primary Mission Weight:	6,554.5 kg (14,450 lb)
Ferry Mission Weight:	9,525.6 kg (21,000 lb)
Maximum Speed:	165 knots
Combat Mission Radius:	209.2 km (130 miles)

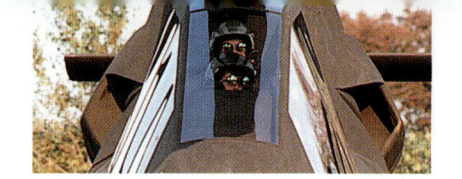

RAH-66 COMANCHE

The Army's newest attack helicopter has been a top priority for the US Army for the past several years. The machine selected to become the first 21st-century attack helicopter will be produced by the team of Boeing-Sikorsky aircraft companies. The *Comanche* is now in full-scale mockup stage, and progressing towards the first prototype.

The *Comanche* is a twin-engined, two-man single main and tail rotor helicopter. The primary mission is reconnaissance, with the capability of being quickly converted to a heavily armed attack helicopter for air-to-ground or air-to-air combat. The *Comanche* is self-contained after being fuelled and armed, and can operate in bad weather and at night without external supporting aircraft.

Since the Vietnam War the Army has utilized two small, lightweight helicopters for scout and reconnaissance work. The Hughes and Bell helicopters have done well and have been kept up to date with advances in electronics equipment. However, the Army has pressed for an armed reconnaissance machine with capabilities that the small scout ships could never meet. That requirement developed into a six-year study and design competition for the Light Attack Helicopter. The team of Boeing and Sikorsky won the award to produce the LH with a neatly laid-out machine designed to fight, win and be maintained with a minimum of manpower.

CONSTRUCTION

The construction of the *Comanche* centres on a composite box beam the length of the fuselage. The rest of the helicopter is attached to this beam in some way. The weapons are all carried by it, as well as the landing gear and the rotor. The tail book is attached to the same beam, as are the engines. The skin of the helicopter is just a skin and has no structural function. This allows the skin to be broken up into doors and access panels anywhere. The skin also is made from composite material and designed to absorb or deflect radar waves. The radar cross-

▼ The AH-66 will be one of the world's fastest pure helicopter with an airspeed of over 200 mph.

▲ **The stealth characteristics of the AH-66 give it an unfamiliar shape.**

section is reported to be about 1% of that of the smaller scout helicopters.

This gunship is classed as a "Light Attack Helicopter", or "LH". It is also referred to as a "Reconnaissance Attack Helicopter" in some publications. It will not supersede the AH-64 *Apache*, but will supplement it. It will replace the current scout machines, and give superior scouting ability to the user. The AH-66 versatility and firepower make it more lethal and more efficient than the present mixture of scouts and gunships. A top speed of over 320 km/h (200 mph) makes the *Comanche* one of the very fastest pure helicopters in the world.

The AH-66 carries 2.5 hours worth of fuel in internal tanks. External tanks can readily be installed to extend the range, which is over 1,930 km (1,200 miles) in a ferry flight. Air refuelling information is not available at this time, but it is expected that this capability will be developed.

Power for the helicopter is supplied by two Garrett and Allison T-800 engines. Each weighs only 136 kg (300 lb), and develops 1,200 shaft horsepower (shp). The engine exhaust is cooled with outside air and ejected through slots along the tail-boom's side. The gas is so cool that heat-seeking missiles will not detect and lock on to it.

STEALTH

The *Comanche*'s airframe is designed for maximum stealth ability and low infra-red signature. The rotor may be made from composite material to reduce the radar cross-section. The weapons are carried on fold-out panels for maximum stealth. Any time the bays are opened the stealth ability is reduced. Wings and weapons that attach to the fuselage also reduce the stealth. The five-bladed main rotor is used to reduce tip speed and noise.

In the armed-reconnaissance role the AH-66 will probably be armed with 500 rounds of 20 mm ammunition for the Gatling gun, four *Hellfire* anti-tank missiles and two *Stinger* air-to-air missiles. The landing gear will be retracted and the weapons bays will be closed for maximum stealth. The *Comanche* avionics package includes precise navigation equipment and a Global Positioning receiver for world-wide navigation. Advanced infra-red vision devices and TV receivers allow the pilots to see in the dark and in bad weather. Nap-of-the-earth flying, very close to the ground, will be the normal mode of operations. Secure radio links will allow intelligence and target hand-off information to be made without compromising the helicopter's location.

Both pilots can view the same, or different, information on two CRT screens in the instrument panel. Vital combat functions and information can be displayed on the see-through visor display attached to the pilot's helmet. Target designation and threat information is also displayed on the helmet-mounted display. The integrated flight control and fire-control system allow the pilot to keep his hands on the side-arm controls at all times and have full control of all systems. Either pilot can aim and fire the turret weapons by means of the helmet-mounted sight, or hand over targets to the other pilot.

Another system, new to attack helicopters, stores a library of infra-red signatures of threat as well as friendly force's vehicles. When a target is detected the system will match the detected signature to the library to aid in identifying the target. A major consideration in night, long-range, anti-tank battles is knowing that the target you are about to launch a *Hellfire* at is an enemy tank, and not a friendly one. There were incidents of mistaken identity during the Gulf War that resulted in the death of friendly forces. This system will reduce incidents of this nature in the future.

Each retractable weapons bay carries three missiles. These can be *Hellfire* or *Stinger* in any combination. Stub wings can be attached to the fuselage

▼ **The AH-66 Comanche carries six missiles in retractable weapons bays.**

SPECIFICATION

DASH SPEED:	Over 320 km/h (200 mph)
INTERNAL FUEL:	2.5 hours
FERRY RANGE:	2,010 km (1,250 miles)
EMPTY WEIGHT:	3,402 kg (7,500 lb)
ARMED RECONNAISSANCE WEIGHT:	4,500+ kg (10,000+ lb)
MAXIMUM WEIGHT:	7,620 kg (16,800 lb)
ENGINES:	Two Garrett and Allison T-800s
MAIN ROTOR:	5 blades, optimized for low-level flight
TAIL ROTOR:	Deducted fan, "Fan-in-fin" type
POWER:	1,200 shp each engine
WEAPONS:	One 20 mm two-barrel cannon
AMMUNITION:	500+ rounds
MISSILES:	Up to 18 *Stinger* air-to-air IR seeking
	Up to 14 *Hellfire* anti-tank laser guided
	Up to 62 *Hydra* 70 mm rockets

▲ The AH-66 full-scale mock-up.

above the weapons bay in about 20 minutes; two pylon stations are available on each wing. Any combination of missiles can be loaded, including up to 14 *Hellfire*, 18 *Stingers* or 62 *Hydra* 70 mm rockets. A reduced weight 20 mm cannon is mounted in the chin turret, and fires 750 or 1,500 rounds per minute.

The AH-66 helicopter has extended range, stealth characteristics and a fully integrated weapons, navigation and flight control package. It is designed to go a long distance, then to find and destroy the enemy. It is the eyes and ears of the Army in the front line and it must survive encounters with the enemy. All of these were the goals of the planners of the Light Attack Helicopter.

▼ The conventional tail rotor has been replaced with a "fan-in-fin" design.

PATRIOT AIR-DEFENCE MISSILE

The *Patriot* is the premier air-defence system in the Western military today. It is a quick-reaction solid-propellent missile capable of intercepting any aircraft in the world today, and tactical ballistic missiles to a limited extent. It is not an anti-ballistic missile (ABM), but an anti-tactical missile (ATM) system. *Patriot* is one of the few modern missile systems to have proved itself in combat.

The design that became the *Patriot* started in the mid-1960s as the SAM-D programme to replace the older NIKE missile system. The competition for the programme was won by the Raytheon Company. The heart of the Raytheon system was, and still is, a Track-via-Missile (TVM) guidance seeker. In this system initial guidance is provided by a ground

▼ **Patriot missile fired against a Lance missile to demonstrate for the first time Patriot's ability to intercept tactical ballistic missiles.**

radar, and as the missile approaches the target on-board seekers provide flight corrections for target interception. The missile does not fly directly at the target, but at a "kill point" that is constantly being computed and corrected. The TVM provides fast, accurate guidance up-dates.

The original SAM-D programme called for an anti-tactical missile capability, but that requirement was dropped soon after the programme started. It was reinstated in 1986 after the initial system was deployed. The *Patriot* computer software was upgraded to support the ATM mission and the first test was to intercept a *Lance* tactical missile. The upgraded system was fielded in 1988 with an active anti-tactical missile capability.

The first SAM-D test successfully engaged a drone target in early 1975. Additional tests proved the ability of the track-via-missile hardware to guide the missile with a very high degree of accuracy. The name was changed to *Patriot* in 1976 and full-scale development proceeded. The first *Patriot* Battalion was activated in May 1982, and was ready for deployment to Europe in 1984. In March 1985 the Battalion was certified and ready for action. Also in 1984–85, The Netherlands and West Germany entered into contracts with Raytheon for additional *Patriot* systems.

When Operation Desert Shield began, *Patriot* units were sent to Saudi Arabia for local air defence. Additional units were dispatched to Turkey and Israel later in the war. On 18 January, 1991, a *Patriot* missile successfully intercepted and destroyed an Iraqi *Scud* tactical ballistic missile fired at Saudi

▼ **The Patriot missile system, shown in the desert environment at White Sands Missile Range, New Mexico. Patriot is designed to counter aircraft, cruise missiles, and tactical ballistic missiles.**

Patriot Missile

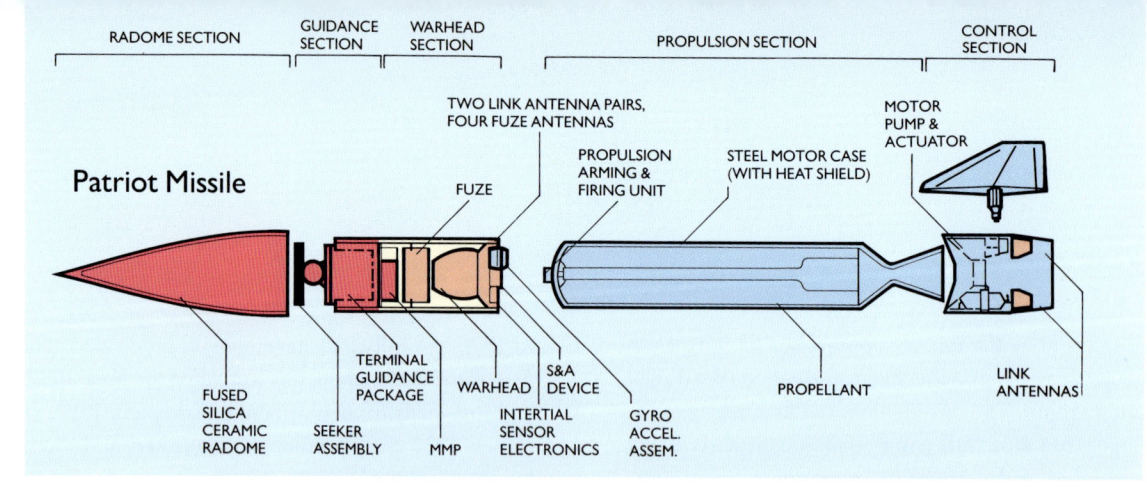

Diagram labels: RADOME SECTION, GUIDANCE SECTION, WARHEAD SECTION, PROPULSION SECTION, CONTROL SECTION; TWO LINK ANTENNA PAIRS, FOUR FUZE ANTENNAS; FUZE; PROPULSION ARMING & FIRING UNIT; STEEL MOTOR CASE (WITH HEAT SHIELD); MOTOR PUMP & ACTUATOR; FUSED SILICA CERAMIC RADOME; SEEKER ASSEMBLY; TERMINAL GUIDANCE PACKAGE; MMP; WARHEAD; INTERTIAL SENSOR ELECTRONICS; S&A DEVICE; GYRO ACCEL. ASSEM.; PROPELLANT; LINK ANTENNAS

Arabia. This marked the first time in history that an air defence system had destroyed a hostile tactical ballistic missile.

During the course of that war at least 43 interceptions were made by *Patriots*. Only one intercept was a failure, and that one resulted in the deaths of several American troops. The *Patriot* system performed far better than was expected, or than the system design called for. The ability to hit a bullet with another bullet has been achieved.

The *Patriot* missile is crated and stored as a "wooden" round. No maintenance is performed on the missile while in storage. The shipping case is also the firing case. The missile box is loaded into position with three other units and tests are made. The status is either fire, or fix. The missile can be fired in single or multi-missile mode. The radar and control centre provide target illumination, target-seeking and missile guidance from the single aerial array.

The *Patriot* motor is a single-stage solid propellant rocket inside a steel case. The four wings on the tail provide what is described as "high-g" manoeuvrability. The motor appears to burn for a long time because some pictures show the flame at time of interception. Altitude, range and speed of the missile are not available at this time. It is obvious that the speed is supersonic, and the altitude must exceed 50,000 ft for effective anti-aircraft interception.

Future developments are being considered to improve the missile, and it is being considered as a future Navy weapon. Shipboard use requires a higher degree of safety than land use. It is also being considered as one layer of a tier for an effective area anti-missile defence system.

It is not possible to provide a perfect umbrella of protection with a single ATM system. The *Patriot* does not, nor has it been claimed to. But it does reduce to a low level the likelihood of damage to the area it defends. Even a multi-tier defence structure may allow some TBMs to get through, although the goal is to reduce it to as near zero as possible.

▼ The Patriot missile system ground radar unit. The entire unit is fully mobile.

SPECIFICATION

Detailed specifications unavailable.

AGM-114 HELLFIRE MISSILE

The *Hellfire* is a modular missile weighing 45.36 kg (100 lb) with a 17.78-cm (7-in) diameter shaped warhead able to destroy the best tanks in the world today. Developed in the 1960s and fielded in the 1980s, it was proved in combat in the Gulf War.

The *Hellfire* (AGM-114) laser-guided missile is the primary weapon carried by the AH-64 *Apache* gunship. The standoff range of the weapon is greater than 4.5 km (5,000 yd). The 7.7-kg (17-lb) warhead has proven lethal. The diameter of a shaped warhead is crucial to the ability of the blast to penetrate the target. The greater the diameter of the explosive, the greater the penetration.

Hellfire missiles may be equipped with different seeker heads for different missions. The most-used has been the laser type, which seeks and tracks a coded laser splash. This laser designator can be in any location, not only on the vehicle carrying the missile. How the coding is accomplished is still classified, but it can quickly be set by both designator and on the missile prior to launch. Once launched, the seeker will search until it acquires the laser splash, than track to the point until impact. The vehicle that launched the missile can be moved as soon as launch is complete.

The next seeker used is an infra-red (focal plane) type. The *Apache* is equipped with night vision devices and infra-red targeting equipment. The IR-seeking head gives the gunship a long-range, very accurate, tank-destroying ability. While it cannot be used in the indirect role, it can be used from any vehicle designed to carry the *Hellfire* as long as the

▼ **A portable launcher with a single missile launch rail and the missile can be set up about anywhere.**

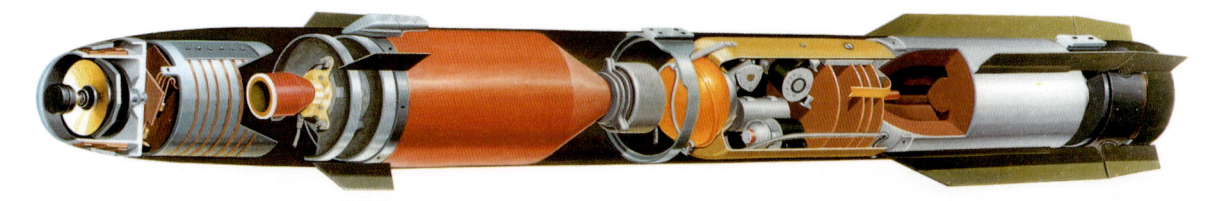

▲ A late model Hellfire, with the small shaped charge in front of the main charge, designed to defeat reactive armour.

gunner can see the target. An improvement to this system is a "stored heat signatures information database" planned for the AH-66 LAH. In this system the IR signature of most possible targets is stored in a computer database in the vehicle. The target is compared to this database to aid in identification of the possible target before the missile is launched.

The missile can also be launched in a rapid fire mode without initial guidance. That is, the missile is fired in such a direction and elevation that it will free fly into an area where its seeker can pick up the laser splash. It will then home in on the target. Multiple missiles (at least eight, perhaps more) can be fired with only one designator to illuminate targets. When the first missile impacts the first target, the designator simply moves to the next target until he runs out of missiles. Present tactics call for eight seconds between missile launches to enable the target shift by the designator. Multiple designators set to different codes mean that a very large number of tanks could all be hit within one minute.

An advantage of the *Hellfire* is that it can be fired from almost any vehicle in a high angle lofting manner to clear hills or other obstructions between launcher and target. The missile then descends in a steep approach and will impact the top of the target.

Tanks are most vulnerable on their top. Range can be greater when a high angle of launch is used, although that range is still classified.

The *Hellfire* can be used in air-to-air combat for defence against other armed helicopters. Although the *Apache* and the new Light Attack Helicopter can be equipped to carry a dedicated air-to-air missile, this *Hellfire* capability reduces the need for dual stores being loaded. The speed of the missile is in excess of Mach 1, so air-to-air use is feasible.

The effectiveness of the *Hellfire* was proved in the Gulf War. One significant engagement was at the end of the ground campaign when retreating Iraqi Republican Guards attacked elements of the 24th Infantry Division. Three companies of the 24th Attack Battalion responded with their *Apache* gunships. In a few hours over 32 tanks and 100 other vehicles were destroyed. This included Iraqi rocket and missile launchers. At least 107 *Hellfire* missiles were launched, with the first launch at a distance of 6,700 m (7,327 yd). At that distance the *Hellfire* was accurate, but the Iraqi tanks had no idea where they were coming from.

An advancement in tank armour has been the addition of "reactive" armour, which explodes when hit and defeats the shaped charge used in anti-tank weapons. To counter this, the *Hellfire* is being improved with the addition of a small shaped charge in the front of the main charge. The theory is that the small charge will set off the reactive armour, and the second main charge can then burn through the target and destroy it.

▼ A Hellfire missile streaks toward the target after being launched from the single rail ground mount launcher.

In future use the *Hellfire* will be mounted in a ground vehicle turret with multiple missiles ready to fire, and reloads inside the vehicle. This system is being developed for the US Army and other countries. It is also being deployed in Sweden as a shore-defence weapon with a single-rail launcher. The Navy is studying the *Hellfire* for shipboard use. A new blast-fragmentation warhead has been developed for anti-ship use. Several different vehicle-mounted systems to carry one to four missiles are under development.

A new seeker, a millimetre-wave seeker known as *Longbow*, is under development for future gunships. It is also being considered for the British Royal Air Force. An advanced digital autopilot is under development so that *Hellfire* can be used from high-speed aircraft. The present missile can be launched from the A-10 tactical support fighter.

The military requirement for a hard-hitting missile with long range and stand-off capability was met in the *Hellfire*. It is not a fire-and-forget weapon because it requires guidance of a sort until impact. However, it does release the launch vehicle from having to remain to guide the missile. Future improvements will give it greater mobility, longer range, and more versatility. The *Hellfire* will be in use for many years.

SPECIFICATION

Length:	162-178 cm (64–70 in)
Weight:	45.81 kg (101 lb)
Diameter:	17.78 cm (7 in)
Speed:	Mach 1+
Seeker:	Laser, Infra-red, Millimetre
Range:	6,700+ m (7,327 yd)
Motor:	Internal burning, solid propellent, low smoke
Warheads:	Conical shaped charge, high explosive anti-tank and Blast Fragmentation with delayed fuse
Launch Vehicles:	Helicopters, attack planes, ground vehicles, portable ground mounts, and ships
Guidance:	Direct with laser and IR, indirect with laser
Warhead Fuse:	Contact, delay or proximity

▲ Hellfire missile launched from an AH-64 Apache gunship.

AGM-65 MAVERICK MISSILE

Maverick is an aircraft launched missile intended for use against a variety of ground targets. These targets include tanks, bunkers, ships and fortifications of all types. The *Maverick* has been employed in combat since October 1973 when the Israeli Air Force described it as ". . . the most successful weapon of the war". The *Maverick* is a true "fire-and-forget" missile system that provides a high probability of kill against these targets.

The initial guidance system was a Television system. With this the pilot's view is actually through the missile, allowing the pilot to lock onto the target prior to launch. After launch the missile's guidance system homes onto the target, allowing the aircraft to turn away. Later versions of the seeker have a magnification system designed to allow an aircraft's pilot to identify the target at a longer range. The later versions have an "Imaging Infra-red" seeker head, or laser seeker. The IIR system provides the pilot with a thermal view of the target area for use during night time and bad weather. Once the missile is launched, no further pilot input is required for the missile to home onto the target. The laser seeker requires that someone maintain a laser designator on the target until impact. The laser designator can be the launch vehicle, another aircraft or a ground based unit.

The *Maverick* can be equipped with various warheads, depending on the target mission. For hard point targets a 59-kg (130-lb) conical shaped charge is carried. The attack with this missile can be carried out from any altitude, even at very low level. The attack altitude determines the angle the missile strikes the target, horizontal or vertical. The 59-kg (130-lb) warhead will completely destroy a tank, and several feet of concrete to get at an aircraft inside a hardened shelter.

▼ **The family of Maverick variants, produced or in the final stages of development.**

SPECIFICATION	
Length:	248.92 cm (98 in)
Diameter:	30.48 cm (12 in)
Wing Span:	72.39 cm (28½ in)
Weight:	209.56-306.18 kg (462–675 lb)
Range:	22.57+ km (14+ miles)
Speed:	Supersonic
Warhead:	59-kg (130-lb) conical shaped or 131.5-kg (290-lb) blast fragmentation
Seeker:	Television, laser or IIR
Guidance:	Fire and forget after target lock on, or laser seeking

The second warhead is a 131.5-kg (290-lb) blast fragmentation unit with a delay fuse that can be set prior to launch. With zero delay the missile is ideal against soft targets in the open, such as radar units or fuel depots. The delay fuse allows the *Maverick* to attack ships, hangars and bunkers covered with earth. The amount of armour the missile will penetrate without breaking up is not available. Pictures of the missile penetrating the side of a double-walled ship and exploding inside have been released. The ship sank.

Maverick is qualified for use on many of the aircraft used by NATO today. An alternative control system is available for those aircraft that do not have a cockpit designed to accept the usual control system. A Navy version is under development to give a low-cost anti-shipping capability along with the large cruise-type missiles.

During the Gulf War the *Maverick* was used in great numbers. Television scenes of missiles striking bunkers and tanks were shown numerous times. The A-10 tactical fighter used many of the missiles with great success against tanks. The A-10 launched them from low altitude most of the time. The number of *Mavericks* launched during the war has not

▲ **A General Dynamics F-16XL test fires one of the six AGM-65 Maverick air-to-surface missiles it was carrying. The airplane was flying at 10,000 feet and Mach .75 when the launch took place.**

yet been released. Production of the *Maverick* has exceeded 30,000 missiles, and they are still in production today.

The *Maverick* guided missile is one of only a few that have proved themselves in combat. With the current development effort, the missile can be expected to improve and be combat capable for many more years.

AIM-120 AMRAAM

The most recent addition to the American air-to-air missile fleet is the AIM-120, AMRAAM. The Advanced Medium Range Air-to-Air Missile is a product of the Hughes Missile Group, Hughes Aircraft Company. It is intended to replace the AIM-7 *Sparrow* as the primary USAF medium-range radar-guided missile for use by all fighter planes.

AMRAAM is designed to improve significantly the air-to-air combat ability of both the US Air Force and the US Navy. The missile is considered to be "state of the art" in missile technology. It incorporates active radar guidance for higher performance, and with modern modernization is one-third smaller and lighter than the *Sparrow*. Maintenance on the missile is reduced, as compared to older systems.

▼ **AIM-120 missiles being prepared for shipment at the Hughes Aircraft Company Tuscon, Arizona, plant's final assembly and check-out facility.**

The AIM-120 is a beyond-visual-range weapon designed for day and night use, and in all weather conditions. Initial guidance is by an inertial reference provided by the aircraft prior to launch. During flight the missile guidance is up-dated by the launch aircraft radar system. The terminal phase of flight is independent of the launch aircraft; the active radar seeker in the missile guides it independently to the target.

Capabilities of the AIM-120 include look down/ shoot down for defence against targets such as low-flying cruise missiles. It has high resistance to electronic counter-measures, and can be used in multiple launch-and-leave tactics. If the targets are within range of the active radar seeker, multiple launches can be made against multiple targets. The launch aircraft can then turn away from the area, leaving the missiles actively seeking the targets.

The missile has also demonstrated the ability to intercept high-flying and high-level manoeuvring targets. Low-flying targets and short-range dogfight targets have also proved

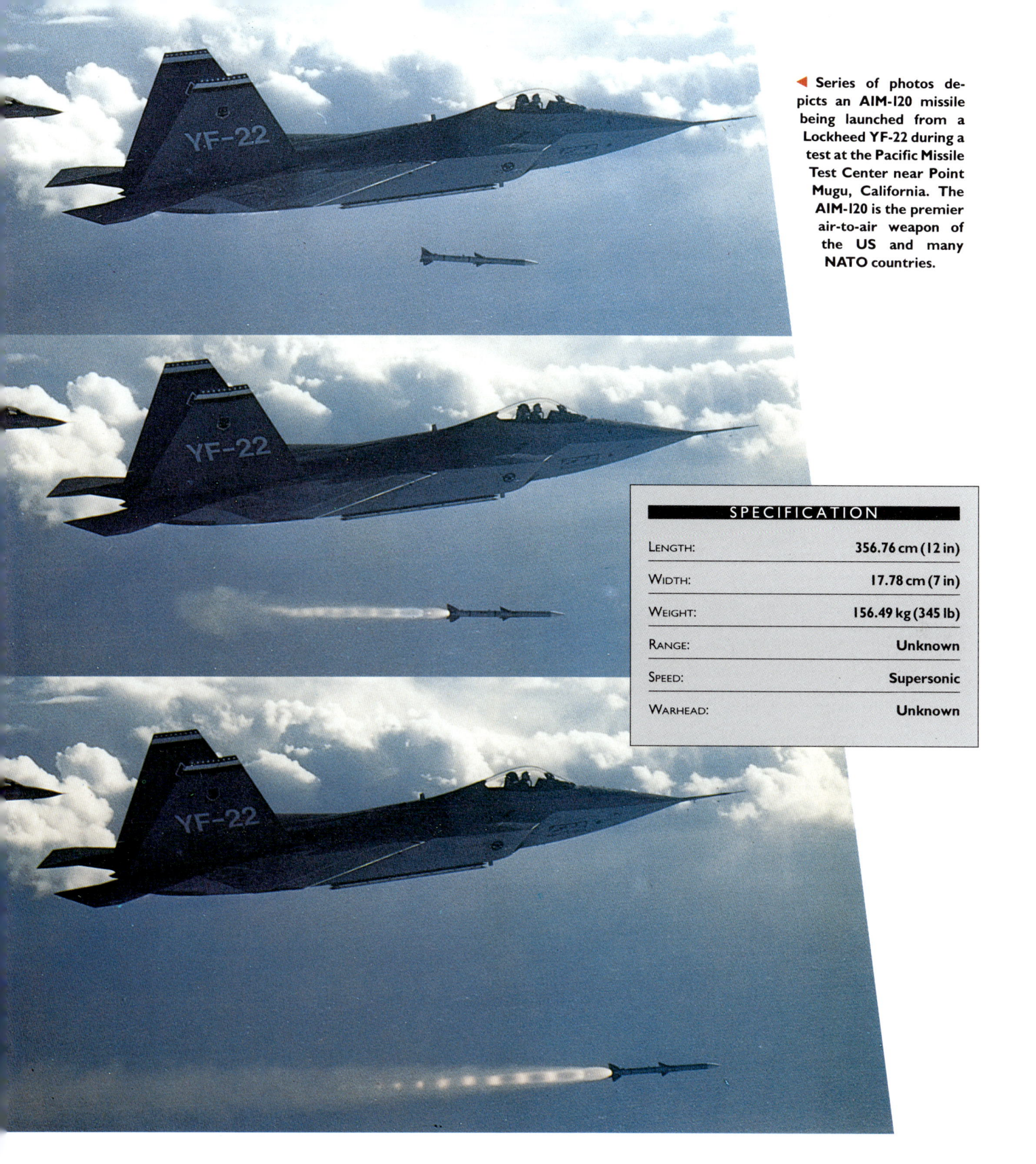

◀ Series of photos depicts an **AIM-120** missile being launched from a Lockheed YF-22 during a test at the Pacific Missile Test Center near Point Mugu, California. The AIM-120 is the premier air-to-air weapon of the US and many NATO countries.

SPECIFICATION	
Length:	356.76 cm (12 in)
Width:	17.78 cm (7 in)
Weight:	156.49 kg (345 lb)
Range:	Unknown
Speed:	Supersonic
Warhead:	Unknown

to be within the ability of the AMRAAM. The goal of a multi-mission medium-range missile seems to have been achieved.

The speed, range and turning ability of the AMRAAM missile is not yet released. It is estimated that the range will be about 96.5 km (60 miles) maximum. The speed is known to be supersonic. To use a missile such as this in a dogfight requires it to have a very high turn rate. Future press releases may compare it to the AIM-9 *Sidewinder*, but we will have to wait for that information.

A low-smoke, high-impulse motor is used to reduce the heat signature of the missile to the aircraft under attack. After motor burn-out the signature is greatly reduced, and the chance of the enemy detecting it is also reduced.

The AMRAAM AIM-120 is being considered as a ship-to-air and a surface-to-air missile system. The future development of the missile seems to be assured.

INDEX

Page numbers in *italics* refer to pictures.

A

A-4 Skyhawk 18
A-7 Corsair 18, 31
A-10 Tactical Support Fighter 107, 108
AA-6 Acid *see* Acid
AA-7 Apex *see* Apex
AA-8 Aphid *see* Aphid
AA-9 Amos *see* Amos
AA-10 Alamo *see* Alamo
AA-11 Archer *see* Archer
AAR-34 8
Aardvark *see* F-111 Aardvark
Acid 39
Advanced Medium Range Air-to-Air
    Missile *see* AMRAAM
Advanced Tactical Fighter *see* F-22
    Advanced Tactical Fighter
Advanced Technology Engines 12
Afghanistan 43
AGM-114 Hellfire Missile *see* Hellfire
AGM-65 Maverick Missile *see* Maverick
AH-1 Cobra 86–90, *86–90*, 91
    S model 87
    specification 90
    Super Cobra *87*, 88, *89*
    weapons 86–8
    Whiskey model *see* Super Cobra
AH-64 Apache 103, *105*, 91–5, *91–5*
    combat 94
    design 91
    specification 95
    weapons 92–3
AIM-120 AMRAAM *see* AMRAAM
AIM-7 Sparrow *see* Sparrow
AIM-9 Sidewinder *see* Sidewinder
AIM-54 Phoenix *see* Phoenix
Air Launched Cruise Missile 53, 55
Airborne Weapons Group Nine *see* AWG-9
Alamo 45, 50
Allison engines
    T406 79
    TF-41 13
ALQ-94 8
ALR-23 8
Amos 48, 50
AMRAAM 20, 29, 82, 108–9, *108–9*
    motor 109
anti-satellite missile (ASAT) 30
anti-tactical missile *see* Patriot Air-
    Defence Missile
Apache *see* AH-64 Apache
Apex 42
APB-65 20
Aphid 42, 45, 50
APQ-110 8
APS-109A 8
Archer 50
ASAT *see* anti-satellite missile
ATM *see* Patriot Air-Defence Missile
AV-8B Harrier 22–6, *22–6*, 76
    air combat 24
    engine 23
    Harrier II 25–6

Harrier II Plus 25
    Sea Harrier 24–5
    specification 26
    weapons 24
avionics *see individual aircraft*
AWG-9 13

B

B-1B Bomber 53–7, *53–7*
    avionics 55
    engines 54
    specification 57
    speed requirement 54
    weapons 55–7
B-1 Bomber *see* B-1B Bomber
B-2 Stealth Bomber 48, 58–61, *58–61*
    combat role 58
    engines 59
    specification 60
    weapons 59–61
B-58 Hustler 38
Backfire bomber 14
Barton, F/Lt. Paul 25
Belenko, Lt. Viktor 39
Bell 76, 91, 96
Benefield, Doug 55
Blackbird *see* SR-71 Blackbird
Blot, Capt. Harry 24
Boeing 53, 62, 76, 96
Boeing 707 Command and Control plane
    21
Boyd, Maj. John 32
British Aerospace 24
Burrows, Irving 28

C

Chapman, Gen. Leonard C 23
Cincinnati Electronics 8
Cobra *see* AH-1 Cobra
Collier Trophy 76
Comanche *see* RAH-66 Comanche
composite materials, use of 59, 67, 68, 96
crew ejection capsule 7

D

Dalmo-Victor 8
Doppler radar 13, 20, 30, 44, 50, 55

E

Eagle *see* F-15 Eagle
ECM *see* electronic counter measures
Egypt 40
electronic counter measures 8
electronic radar suppression 31
energy manoeuvrability 32
engines *see individual manufacturers and
    aircraft*

F

F-4 Phantom 6, 13, 14, 18, 27, 31, 42
F-14 Tomcat 6, 11–17, *11–17*, 18, 27,
    35, 43
    avionics and electronics 13
    performance and handling 15

    power plant 12
    specification 16
    structure 11
    weapons 14
F-15 Eagle 27–31, *27–31*, 32, 36, 38
    armament 29
    combat operation 30
    control 29
    performance 29–30
    specification 31
    Strike Eagle 29
F-16 Fighting Falcon 18, 21, 32–6, *32–6*
    first combat 36
    handling 34–5
    performance 34–5
    specification 36
F-17 32
F-20 Tigershark 35
F-22 Advanced Tactical Fighter 62–7,
    62–7
    avionics 63
    compared to F-15 63, 67
    competition with F-23 62
    engines 67
    specifications 65
    weapons 62
F-23 Northrop Fighter *see* YF-23 Northrop
    Fighter
F-104 Starfighter 20, 32, 54
F-105 Thunderchief 6
F-111 Aardvark 11, 31, 6–10, *6–10*
    avionics 8
    cancellation of programme 7
    engines 7
    programme 53
    specification 9
    weapons 10
F-117 Stealth Fighter 58, 72–5, *72–5*
    combat 73–4
    secrecy of project 73
    specification 75
    weapons 72
F/A-18 Hornet 18–21, *18–21*, 35
    cockpit 19
    controls 19
    performance 21
    power plants 20
    radar and sensors 20
    specification 21
    weapons 20
Falkland Islands operation 24–5
FFAR 92
fibre optics 63
Fighter-Experimental *see* FX (Fighter-
    Experimental)
Fighting Falcon *see* F-16 Fighting Falcon
Fire Control Computer (FCC) 87, 92
Flanker *see* Su-27 Flanker
FLIR *see* forward looking infra-red
Flogger *see* MiG-23 Flogger
fly-by-wire 12, 19, 29, 33, 45, 50, 67, 72
Folding Fin Aerial Rocket *see* FFAR
forward looking infra-red (FLIR) 20
Foxbat *see* MiG-25 Foxbat

Foxhound *see* MiG-31 Foxhound
Fulcrum *see* MiG-29 Fulcrum
FX (Fighter-Experimental) 27

G
Gadhafi, Col. Moamar al 10, 40
Garrett and Allison T-800 engine 97
Gatling gun 97
General Dynamics 62
General Dynamics F-16 Fighting Falcon *see* F-16 Fighting Falcon
General Dynamics F-111 Aardvark *see* F-111 Aardvark
General Electric 31
General Electric engines
    F-101 13, 54
    F-118 59
    F-404 18, 20, 72
    JY-101 20
    T700 92
    TP-30 12
    YF120 67
Glover, F/Lt. Jeffrey 25
Grumman F-14 Tomcat *see* F-14 Tomcat
Gulf War 14, *20*, 27, 30, 35, 73, *87*, 88, 89, 94–5, *95*, 98, 104, 107
Guryevich, Mikhail 37

H
HARM *see* High Speed Anti-Radiation Missile
Harpoon 20
Harrier *see* AV-8B Harrier
Harrier II *see* AV-8B Harrier
Harrier II Plus *see* AV-8B Harrier
Hawk 39
Hawker Siddeley 24
Hawkeye 21
Heads Up Display 19, 25, 30, 35, 50
Hellfire 88, 92–3, 97, 98, 103–5, *103–5*
    air-to-air use 104
    future uses 105
helmet-mounted sight 87, 92, 98
High Lark radar 42
High Speed Anti-Radiation Missile 20
Hornet *see* F/A-18 Hornet
HUD *see* Heads Up Display
Hughes 13, 91, 96, 108
Hunter 22
Hydra *94*

I J K
Imaging Infra-red Seeker 106
Israel 30, 36, 40, 43
Johnson, Kelly 80, 81
Kestrel 22
Korea 86

L
Langley Laboratory 6
Larx 44, *45*
laser designator 103, 106
laser spot tracking 20
Lewis, Gordon 22
Libya 10, 43; *see also* Gadhafi, Col. Mosmar al
Light Weight Fighter (LWF) competition 18
Lockheed 62, 72, 80
Longbow 105
look down/shoot down 37, 108

Lycoming T-53 87

M
Maverick 20, 25, 29, 34, 106–7, *106–7*
    specification 107
    warheads 106–7
McDonnell Douglas AV-8B Harrier *see* AV-8B Harrier
McDonnell Douglas F-15 Eagle *see* F-15 Eagle
McNamara, Robert S. 6, 11
Middle East conflict *see* Gulf War
MiG-21 33, 36, *37*
MiG-23 Flogger 36, 40, 41–3
    combat 43
    engines 41–2
    MiG-27 variant 42, 43
    weapons 42
MiG-25 Foxbat 13, 38–40, *38–40*, 44, 47
    combat role 39–40
    engines 38
    specification 40
    weapons 39
MiG-27 Flogger 42, 43
    variations from MiG-23 42
    see also MiG-23 Flogger
MiG-29 Fulcrum 33, 44–6, *44–6*, 62
    engines 45–6
    specification 46
    weapons 44–5
MiG-31 Foxhound 47–9, *47–9*
    avionics 47–8
    combat 48
    engines 48
    specification 49
MiGs 27
    overview 37
    early models 37
Mikoyan, Artem 37
Mikoyan and Guryevich 37
Mirage 25
multiplexing 55

N
Night Vision Sensor 93
Northrop F/A-18 Hornet *see* F/A-18 Hornet
Northrop Fighter *see* YF-23 Northrop Fighter
nuclear weapons 6, 10, 38, 55, 57, 59, 85

O
Oestricher, Phil 33
Operation Desert Shield *see* Gulf War
Osirak nuclear reactor 36
Osprey *see* V-22 Osprey

P
P-51 Mustang 32
P1127 22
Packard, David A 32
Patriot Air-Defence Missile 100–102, *100–102*
    future developments 102
    motor 102
Pegasus 22, 25
Phalanx shell 89
Phantom *see* F-4 Phantom
Phoenix 13, 14, 15
Pratt and Whitney 31
Pratt and Whitney engines

F-100 29, 33
F-401 13
J-58 81
J-75 81
TF30 7
YF119 67
pulse-Doppler radar *see* Doppler radar

R
R-23 BVR 42
R-60 42
RAH-66 Comanche 96–9, *96–9*
    avionics 97–8
    construction 96–7
    specification 98
    stealth 97
    weapons 98–9
Rapier 14
Raytheon Company 100
reactive armour 104
Republic F105 Thunderchif *see* F105 Thunderchief
Rockwell International 53
Royal Air Force 25
Royal Navy 24

S
SA-6 SAM 8
SAM-D programme 100–101
Sanders Associates 8
Schalk, Lou 81
Shlesinger, James R. 33
Scud 101–2
Sea Harrier *see* AV-8B Harrier
Seamans Jr, Robert G. 28
Short Range Attack Missile *see* SRAM
short take off (STO) 23
Sidewinder 13, 14, 15, 20, 25, 27, 34, 68, 89
Sikorsky 96
ski-jump 24
Sparrow 13, 14, 15, 20, 29, 34, 108
spin button 19
spring-and-bobweight system 12
SR-71 Blackbird 80–5, *80–5*
    construction 80–1
    design 83
    engines 81–3
    heat problems 81, 83
    specification 84
    YF-12A 85
SRAM 53, 55
Stack, John 6
Stealth Bomber *see* B-2 Stealth Bomber
Stealth Fighter *see* F-117 Stealth Fighter
stealth technology 58–61, 62, 68, 72–5, 97
Stinger 43, 89, 97, 98
STO *see* short take off
Strike Eagle *see* F-15 Eagle
Su-22 36
Su-27 Flanker 50–2, *50–2*
    avionics 50–1
    specification 52
    weapons 50–51
Super Cobra *see* AH-1 Cobra
Syrian aircraft 30, 36, 40

T
tailerons 12
Target Acquisition and Designation Sight

(TADS) 92, 93
Taylor, Lt. Cdr. Doug 24
Taylor, Lt. Nick 25
Telescopic Sighting Unit 87
terrain-following radar 6, 8
Texas Instruments 8
Thailand 10
thrust vectoring *31*, 63
Tiltrotor team 76
titanium, use of 38, 45, 47, 80–1
Tomahawk cruise missile 74
Tomcat *see* F-14 Tomcat
Tornado 48
TOW 87, 88
Track-via-Missile (TVM) 100–101
Tube-launched Optical-tracked Wire-guided missile *see* TOW
Tumansky engines
   R-27 42
   R-29 42
   R-31 38–9
   R-33 46
TVM *see* Track-via-Missile

U V

US Marine Corps 23, 76
US Navy *11*, *15*, *27*, *33*, *67*, 77
V-22 Osprey 76–9, *76–9*
   civilian uses 76–7
   design 76
   engines 79
   naval use 77, 79
   rotors 78–9
   specification 78
variable geometry wings 6–7, *7*, 11, *41*
variable sweep wing *see* variable geometry wing
Vector In Forward Flight *see* VIFFing
vertical take off and landing (VTOL) *23*, 76
Very High Speed Integrated Circuits 63
VFX (Experimental Fighter) competition 11
VG *see* variable geometry wings
Vickers 6
Vietnam War 10, 27, 42, 86, 91
VIFFing 24
VTOL *see* vertical take off and landing
Vulcan cannon 10, 13, 20, 29, 33

W

Wibault, Michel 22, 25
Wild Weasel 31
wing-root extension *see* Larx

X Y

XB-70 38
YF-12A 85
YF-17 18
YF-23 Northrop Fighter 68–71, *68–71*
   competition with F-22 62
   specifications 71

PICTURE CREDITS

The publisher would like to thank the following for supplying photographs used in this book and for permission to use them.

Bell Helicopter Textron 77 B & T, 79, 86, 87, 89 B & T, 90 T. **Bob Archer** 38, 39 B, 40, 41. **Chris Dymond** 46 T, 91 B. **Foto Consortium:** Alain Ernoult 45 T, 50, 51 T, 52 T, B; Kirby Harrison 15; Gary L. Keiffer 9, 44, 51 B, 46 B; Peter R. March 42 B, 43, 47; Frank Mormillo 11, 12, 34 T; Mi D. Seitelman 16, 32, 53, 54, 55, 56, 88; Leif Skoogfors 76, 78; 14 T, 39 T, 97. **Grumman** 14. **Hughes** 106, 107, 108, 109. **Lockheed** 62, 63 B & T, 64, 66, 67, 74, 75 B, 80, 82, 83. **McDonnell Douglas** 18, 19 B & T, 21 B & T, 22, 23 B & T, 24, 25, 26, 29, 30, 31 B & T, 92 B & T, 93, 95 B & T. **Novosti** 48. **Quadrant** 49. **Rockwell International** 103, 104 B & T, 105. **Sikorsky** 96, 98, 99 B & T. **Schultzinger and Lombard** 72, 75 TL & TR. **US Air Force** 10, 27, 58, 59, 60, 61, 68 B & T, 69, 70, 73. **US Department of Defense** 13, 84.

Every effort has been made to trace all copyright holders. The publisher would like to apologise if any omissions have been made.